PRACTICE — ASSESS — DIAGNOSE

180 Days of READING
for Second Grade

Author

Christine Dugan, M.A.Ed.

Shell
Education

Publishing Credits

Dona Herweck Rice, *Editor-in-Chief;* Robin Erickson, *Production Director;*
Lee Aucoin, *Creative Director;* Timothy J. Bradley, *Illustration Manager;*
Conni Medina, M.A.Ed., *Editorial Director;* Sara Johnson, M.S.Ed., *Senior Editor;*
Aubrie Nielsen, M.S.Ed., *Editor;* Grace Alba, *Designer;* Maple Lam, *Illustrator;*
Stephanie Reid, *Photo Editor;* Corinne Burton, M.A.Ed., *Publisher*

Image Credits

Cover, Maple Lam; p. 96 Newscom; p. 144 NASA; p. 216 Getty images; all other images Shutterstock

Standards

© 2007 Teachers of English to Speakers of Other Languages, Inc. (TESOL)
© 2007 Board of Regents of the University of Wisconsin System. World-Class Instructional Design and Assessment
(WIDA). For more information on using the WIDA ELP Standards, please visit the WIDA website at www.wida.us.
© 2010 National Governors Association Center for Best Practices and Council of Chief State School Officers (CCSS)

Shell Education

5482 Argosy Avenue
Huntington Beach, CA 92649-1030
www.tcmpub.com/shell-education

ISBN 978-1-4258-0923-2

©2013 Shell Education Publishing, Inc.

TABLE OF CONTENTS

INTRODUCTION AND RESEARCH

The Need for Practice

In order to be successful in today's reading classroom, students must deeply understand both concepts and procedures so that they can discuss and demonstrate their understanding. Demonstrating understanding is a process that must be continually practiced in order for students to be successful. According to Marzano, "practice has always been, and always will be, a necessary ingredient to learning procedural knowledge at a level at which students execute it independently" (2010, 83). Practice is especially important to help students apply reading comprehension strategies and word-study skills.

Understanding Assessment

In addition to providing opportunities for frequent practice, teachers must be able to assess students' comprehension and word-study skills. This is important so that teachers can adequately address students' misconceptions, build on their current understanding, and challenge them appropriately. Assessment is a long-term process that often involves careful analysis of student responses from a lesson discussion, a project, a practice sheet, or a test. When analyzing the data, it is important for teachers to reflect on how their teaching practices may have influenced students' responses and to identify those areas where additional instruction may be required. In short, the data gathered from assessments should be used to inform instruction: slow down, speed up, or reteach. This type of assessment is called *formative assessment*.

HOW TO USE THIS BOOK

180 Days of Reading for Second Grade offers teachers and parents a full page of daily reading comprehension and word-study practice activities for each day of the school year.

Easy to Use and Standards Based

These activities reinforce grade-level skills across a variety of reading concepts. The questions are provided as a full practice page, making them easy to prepare and implement as part of a classroom morning routine, at the beginning of each reading lesson, or as homework.

Every second-grade practice page provides questions that are tied to a reading or writing standard. Students are given the opportunity for regular practice in reading comprehension and word study, allowing them to build confidence through these quick standards-based activities.

Question	College and Career Readiness Standards
Days 1–3	
1–2	**Reading Anchor Standard 1:** *Read closely to determine what the text says explicitly and to make logical inferences from it* **or** **Reading Anchor Standard 2:** *Determine central ideas or themes of a text and analyze their development; summarize the key supporting details and ideas.*
3	**Reading Foundational Skills Standard:** *Know and apply grade-level phonics and word analysis skills in decoding words.*
4	**Reading Anchor Standard 4:** *Interpret words and phrases as they are used in a text, including determining technical, connotative, and figurative meanings, and analyze how specific word choices shape meaning or tone.*
Day 4	
1	**Reading Anchor Standard 1:** *Read closely to determine what the text says explicitly and to make logical inferences from it.*
2–3	**Reading Anchor Standard 10:** *Read and comprehend complex literary and informational texts independently and proficiently.*
4–5	**Reading Anchor Standard 2:** *Determine central ideas or themes of a text and analyze their development; summarize the key supporting details and ideas.*
Day 5	
	Writing Anchor Standard 4: *Produce clear and coherent writing in which the development, organization, and style are appropriate to task, purpose, and audience.*

HOW TO USE THIS BOOK (cont.)

Using the Practice Pages

Practice pages provide instruction and assessment opportunities for each day of the school year. The activities are organized into weekly themes, and teachers may wish to prepare packets of each week's practice pages for students. Days 1, 2, and 3 follow a consistent format, with a short piece of text and four corresponding items. As outlined on page 4, every item is aligned to a reading standard.

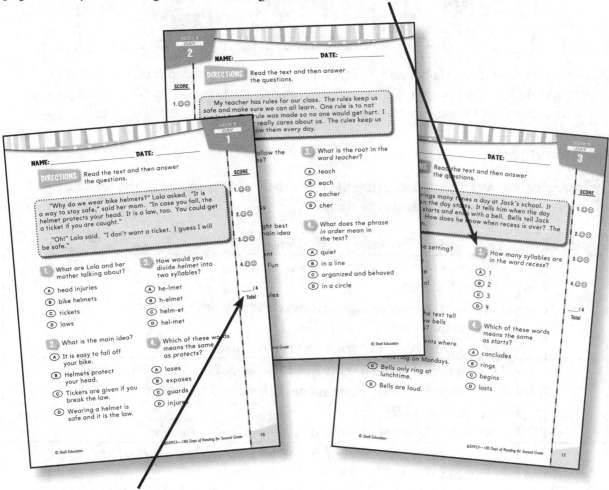

Using the Scoring Guide

Use the scoring guide along the side of each practice page to check answers and see at a glance which skills may need more reinforcement.

Fill in the appropriate circle for each problem to indicate correct (☺) or incorrect (☹) responses. You might wish to indicate only incorrect responses to focus on those skills. (For example, if students consistently miss items 2 and 4, they may need additional help with those concepts as outlined in the table on page 4.) Use the answer key at the back of the book to score the problems, or you may call out answers to have students self-score or peer-score their work.

HOW TO USE THIS BOOK (cont.)

 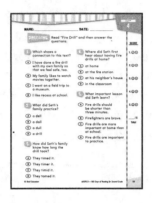 

A longer text is used for Days 4 and 5. Students answer more in-depth comprehension questions on Day 4 and complete a written response to the text on Day 5. This longer text can also be used for fluency practice (see page 7).

Writing Rubric

Score students' written responses using the rubric below. Display the rubric for students to reference as they write (G2_writing_rubric.pdf).

Points	Criteria
4	• Uses an appropriate organizational sequence to produce very clear and coherent writing • Uses descriptive language that develops or clarifies ideas • Engages the reader • Uses a style very appropriate to task, purpose, and audience
3	• Uses an organizational sequence to produce clear and coherent writing • Uses descriptive language that develops or clarifies ideas • Engages the reader • Uses a style appropriate to task, purpose, and audience
2	• Uses an organizational sequence to produce somewhat clear and coherent writing • Uses some descriptive language that develops or clarifies ideas • Engages the reader in some way • Uses a style somewhat appropriate to task, purpose, and audience
1	• Does not use an organized sequence; the writing is not clear or coherent • Uses little descriptive language to develop or clarify ideas • Does not engage the reader • Does not use a style appropriate to task, purpose, or audience
0	Offers no writing or does not respond to the assignment presented

HOW TO USE THIS BOOK *(cont.)*

Developing Students' Fluency Skills

What Is Fluency?

According to the National Reading Panel Report, there are five critical factors that are vital to effective reading instruction: phonemic awareness, phonics, fluency, vocabulary, and comprehension (2000). Rasinski (2006) defines fluency as "the ability to accurately and effortlessly decode the written words and then to give meaning to those words through appropriate phrasing and oral expression of the words." Wolf (2005) notes that the goal of developing fluency is comprehension rather than the ability to read rapidly. Becoming a fluent reader is a skill that develops gradually and requires practice. Reading text repeatedly with a different purpose each time supports the development of fluency in young children (Rasinski 2003).

Assessing Fluency

Fluent readers read accurately, with expression, and at a good pace. A Fluency Rubric along with detailed instructions for scoring and keeping oral reading records is included in the digital resources (G2_fluency.pdf).

The table below lists fluency norms by grade level (Rasinski 2003):

Student Fluency Norms Based On Words Correct Per Minute (WCPM)			
Grade	Fall	Winter	Spring
1	—	—	60 wcpm
2	53	78	94
3	79	93	114
4	99	112	118
5	105	118	128
6	115	132	145

HOW TO USE THIS BOOK *(cont.)*

Diagnostic Assessment

Teachers can use the practice pages as diagnostic assessments. The data analysis tools included with the book enable teachers or parents to quickly score students' work and monitor their progress. Teachers and parents can see at a glance which reading concepts or skills students may need to target in order to develop proficiency.

After students complete a practice page, grade each page using the answer key (pages 231–237). Then, complete the Practice Page Item Analysis for the appropriate day (pages 10–11) for the whole class, or the Student Item Analysis (pages 12–13) for individual students. These charts are also provided in the digital resources (filenames: G2_practicepage_analysis.pdf, G2_student_analysis.pdf). Teachers can input data into the electronic files directly on the computer, or they can print the pages and analyze students' work using paper and pencil.

To complete the Practice Page Item Analyses:

- Write or type students' names in the far-left column. Depending on the number of students, more than one copy of the form may be needed, or you may need to add rows.

- The item numbers are included across the top of the charts. Each item correlates with the matching question number from the practice page.

- For each student, record an *X* in the column if the student has the item incorrect. If the item is correct, leave the item blank.

- Count the *X*s in each row and column and fill in the correct boxes.

To complete the Student Item Analyses:

- Write or type the student's name on the top row. This form tracks the ongoing progress of each student, so one copy per student is necessary.

- The item numbers are included across the top of the chart. Each item correlates with the matching question number from the practice page.

- For each day, record an *X* in the column if the student has the item incorrect. If the item is correct, leave the item blank.

- Count the *X*s in each row and column and fill in the correct boxes.

HOW TO USE THIS BOOK (cont.)

Using the Results to Differentiate Instruction

Once results are gathered and analyzed, teachers can use the results to inform the way they differentiate instruction. The data can help determine which concepts are the most difficult for students and which need additional instructional support and continued practice. Depending on how often the practice pages are scored, results can be considered for instructional support on a daily or weekly basis.

Whole-Class Support

The results of the diagnostic analysis may show that the entire class is struggling with a particular concept or group of concepts. If these concepts have been taught in the past, this indicates that further instruction or reteaching is necessary. If these concepts have not been taught in the past, this data is a great preassessment and demonstrates that students do not have a working knowledge of the concepts. Thus, careful planning for the length of the unit(s) or lesson(s) must be considered, and extra frontloading may be required.

Small-Group or Individual Support

The results of the diagnostic analysis may show that an individual or small group of students is struggling with a particular concept or group of concepts. If these concepts have been taught in the past, this indicates that further instruction or reteaching is necessary. Consider pulling aside these students while others are working independently to instruct further on the concept(s). Teachers can also use the results to help identify individuals or groups of proficient students who are ready for enrichment or above-grade-level instruction. These students may benefit from independent-learning contracts or more challenging activities. Students may also benefit from extra practice using games or computer-based resources.

Digital Resources

Reference page 239 for information about accessing the digital resources and an overview of the contents.

PRACTICE PAGE ITEM ANALYSIS DAYS 1-3

Directions: Record an X in cells to indicate where students have missed questions. Add up the totals. You can view the following: (1) which items were missed per student; (2) the total correct score for each student; and (3) the total number of students who missed each item.

Week: _____ Day: _____

Student Name	Item #					# correct
		1	2	3	4	
Sample Student			X			3/4
# of students missing each question						

PRACTICE PAGE ITEM ANALYSIS DAYS 4-5

Directions: Record an *X* in cells to indicate where students have missed questions. Add up the totals. You can view the following: (1) which items were missed per student; (2) the total correct score for each student; and (3) the total number of students who missed each item.

Week: _____ Day: _____

Student Name	Item # 1	2	3	4	5	# correct	Written Response
Sample Student		X			X	3/5	3
# of students missing each question							Written Response Average:

STUDENT ITEM ANALYSIS DAYS 1-3

Directions: Record an *X* in cells to indicate where the student has missed questions. Add up the totals. You can view the following: (1) which items the student missed; (2) the total correct score per day; and (3) the total number of times each item was missed.

Student Name: Sample Student						
Item		1	2	3	4	# correct
Week	Day					
1	1		X			3/4
	Total					

STUDENT ITEM ANALYSIS DAYS 4-5

Directions: Record an *X* in cells to indicate where the student has missed questions. Add up the totals. You can view: (1) which items the student missed; (2) the total correct score per day; and (3) the total number of times each item was missed.

Student Name: **Sample Student**							Day 5
	Day 4						
Item	1	2	3	4	5	# correct	**Written Response**
Week							
1		X			X	3/5	*3*
Total							
							Written Response Average:

STANDARDS CORRELATIONS

Shell Education is committed to producing educational materials that are research and standards based. In this effort, we have correlated all of our products to the academic standards of all 50 United States, the District of Columbia, the Department of Defense Dependent Schools, and all Canadian provinces.

How To Find Standards Correlations

To print a customized correlation report of this product for your state, visit our website at **www.tcmpub.com/shell-education** and follow the on-screen directions. If you require assistance in printing correlation reports, please contact Customer Service at 1-877-777-3450.

Purpose and Intent of Standards

Legislation mandates that all states adopt academic standards that identify the skills students will learn in kindergarten through grade twelve. Many states also have standards for Pre-K. This same legislation sets requirements to ensure the standards are detailed and comprehensive.

Standards are designed to focus instruction and guide adoption of curricula. Standards are statements that describe the criteria necessary for students to meet specific academic goals. They define the knowledge, skills, and content students should acquire at each level. Standards are also used to develop standardized tests to evaluate students' academic progress. Teachers are required to demonstrate how their lessons meet state standards. State standards are used in the development of all of our products, so educators can be assured they meet the academic requirements of each state.

College and Career Readiness

The activities in this book are aligned to the college and career readiness (CCR) standards. The chart on page 4 lists each standard that is addressed in this product.

TESOL and WIDA Standards

The activities in this book promote English language development for English language learners.

NAME:_____ **DATE:**_____

DIRECTIONS Read the text and then answer the questions.

"Why do we wear bike helmets?" Lola asked.

"It is a way to stay safe," said her mom. "If you fall, the helmet will protect your head. It is a law, too. You could get a ticket if you are caught riding without a helmet."

"Oh!" Lola said. "I don't want a ticket. I guess I will be safe."

1. ☺ ☹

2. ☺ ☹

3. ☺ ☹

4. ☺ ☹

____ / 4
Total

1. What are Lola and her mom talking about?

Ⓐ head injuries

Ⓑ bike helmets

Ⓒ tickets

Ⓓ laws

2. What is the main idea?

Ⓐ It is easy to fall off your bike.

Ⓑ Helmets protect your head.

Ⓒ Tickets are given if you break the law.

Ⓓ Wearing a helmet is safe and it is the law.

3. How would the word *helmet* be divided into two syllables?

Ⓐ he-lmet

Ⓑ h-elmet

Ⓒ helm-et

Ⓓ hel-met

4. Which of these words means the same as *protect*?

Ⓐ lose

Ⓑ expose

Ⓒ guard

Ⓓ injure

NAME:_____ DATE:_____

DIRECTIONS Read the text and then answer the questions.

SCORE

1. ☺ ☹

2. ☺ ☹

3. ☺ ☹

4. ☺ ☹

___ / 4
Total

My teacher has rules for our class. The rules keep us safe and make sure we can all learn. One rule is to not run inside. This rule was made so no one would get hurt. I think my teacher really cares about us. The rules keep us in order, so I follow them every day.

1. Who has to follow the teacher's rules?

(A) the student

(B) the teacher

(C) the principal

(D) the whole class

2. Which title best fits the text?

(A) A Caring Student

(B) Running Is Not Fun

(C) Keeping Order with Rules

(D) Breaking the Rules

3. What is the root word in *teacher*?

(A) teach

(B) each

(C) eacher

(D) cher

4. What does the phrase *in order* mean in the text?

(A) quiet

(B) in a line

(C) organized and behaved

(D) in a circle

NAME:_____ **DATE:**_____

DIRECTIONS Read the text and then answer the questions.

   The bell rings many times a day at Jack's school. It tells him when the day starts. It tells him when the day ends. Lunch starts and ends with a bell. Bells tell Jack where to go. How does he know when recess is over? The bell alerts him.

1. ☺ ☹

2. ☺ ☹

3. ☺ ☹

4. ☺ ☹

1. What is the setting?

(A) Jack's bike

(B) Jack's home

(C) Jack's school

(D) Jack's room

2. How do bells help students?

(A) Bells tell students where to go.

(B) Bells ring on Mondays.

(C) Bells only ring at lunchtime.

(D) Bells are loud.

3. How many syllables are in the word *recess*?

(A) one syllable

(B) two syllables

(C) three syllables

(D) four syllables

____ / 4
Total

4. Which of these words means the same as *starts*?

(A) concludes

(B) rings

(C) begins

(D) lasts

NAME:_____ DATE:_____

Fire Drill

Seth learned about fire drills at school. His class went on a field trip to the fire station. The firefighters talked to the students about safety. Schools have fire drills to prepare students for a fire. The firefighters told the students that they should have fire drills at home, too.

Seth went home and told his parents what he learned. His family decided to try a fire drill. First, they tested their smoke alarms. They wanted to make sure that the alarms were still working. Then, they pretended that an alarm went off. They got out of their house, and they timed the drill. It took them three minutes. They all agreed they could do better. They would try again.

Seth was happy. He felt safe. He was glad his family had done a fire drill. He knew the firefighters would be proud.

NAME:_____ **DATE:**_____

DIRECTIONS Read "Fire Drill" and then answer the questions.

1. Which shows a connection to this text?

(A) I have done a fire drill with my own family so I feel safe, too.

(B) My family likes to watch movies together.

(C) I went on a field trip to a museum.

(D) I like recess at school.

2. What did Seth's family practice?

(A) a dell

(B) a doll

(C) a dull

(D) a drill

3. How did Seth's family know how long the drill took?

(A) They timed it.

(B) They timer it.

(C) They timid it.

(D) They tamed it.

4. Where did Seth first hear about having fire drills at home?

(A) at home

(B) at the fire station

(C) at his neighbor's house

(D) in the classroom

5. What important lesson did Seth learn?

(A) Fire drills should be shorter than three minutes.

(B) Firefighters are brave.

(C) Fire drills are more important at home than at school.

(D) Fire drills are important to practice.

1. ☺ ☺

2. ☺ ☺

3. ☺ ☺

4. ☺ ☺

5. ☺ ☺

____ / 5
Total

NAME: _____ **DATE:** _____

 Reread the text "Fire Drill."

 Think about some of the ways that you are safe with your own family.

✏️ **Write about** one thing your family does to stay safe.

_____

_____

_____

_____

_____

_____

_____

_____

_____

_____

_____

NAME:_____ DATE:_____

DIRECTIONS Read the text and then answer the questions.

Surfing is a very fun sport for people who enjoy thrilling rides. Surfers ride waves on their surfboards. They learn how to stand up. They ride the best parts of a wave. They are always looking for a fun ride!

1. What is the main topic?

A sports

B the ocean

C waves

D surfing

2. According to this text, who enjoys surfing?

A people who live near the ocean

B people who can swim

C people who are looking for a thrilling ride

D people who can stand up

3. Which of these words from the text is a compound word?

A thrilling

B looking

C surfboards

D surfers

4. What does the word *thrilling* mean?

A very exciting

B wet

C scary

D water

NAME:_____ DATE:_____

DIRECTIONS Read the text and then answer the questions.

Lifeguards make sure that beaches are safe. Some days, it is too rough to swim in the ocean. The waves are too big. Lifeguards fly a flag. A double red flag lets people know the beach is closed. The ocean is very powerful. Even the strongest swimmers cannot swim in huge waves.

1. Which title best fits the text?

(A) Lifeguard Training

(B) Staying Safe at the Beach

(C) Flying Flags

(D) More Huge Waves

2. What is a lifeguard's main job?

(A) to watch huge waves

(B) to swim in the ocean

(C) to fly flags

(D) to make sure the beach is safe

3. What is the root word in *powerful*?

(A) owe

(B) power

(C) wer

(D) ful

4. Which of these things might be considered *too rough*?

(A) jumping on the bed

(B) swinging high on the swings

(C) a hard push in a game of tag

(D) a soccer goal

#50923—180 Days of Reading for Second Grade

NAME:_____ **DATE:**_____

DIRECTIONS Read the text and then answer the questions.

Shark attacks are scary. Most sharks eat meat. They like large fish or seals. They do not hunt humans, but attacks do happen. Attacks are very rare. Sharks may bite a person swimming in the ocean. They may think they are eating a seal.

1. ☺ ☹

2. ☺ ☹

3. ☺ ☹

4. ☺ ☹

____ / 4
Total

1. What is this text mostly about?

(A) seals

(B) shark attacks

(C) the ocean

(D) shark food

2. What does this text **not** say about shark attacks on humans?

(A) Shark sometimes mistake humans for food.

(B) They are scary.

(C) They happen in warm water.

(D) They are rare.

3. Which word has the same root word as *eating*?

(A) each

(B) eaten

(C) at

(D) tingly

4. Which words from the text have similar meanings?

(A) *rare* and *scary*

(B) *like* and *bite*

(C) *attack* and *hunt*

(D) *think* and *like*

NAME:_____   DATE:_____

Investigating Tide Pools

Tide pools are small, rocky pools. They are found on the beach. They fill with water at high tide. At low tide, the water goes away. People can then walk to them. Plants and animals live inside.

A tide pool is a unique habitat. The organisms must survive in high and low tides. They are at great risk. They might be swept away by the ocean. Seagulls like to snack on tide pool creatures. Too much sun can dry them out, too.

Starfish live in tide pools. Starfish come in a variety of sizes and colors. They like to eat mussels. A starfish wants a mussel before a gull eats it instead!

Anemones (uh-NEM-uh-neez) also live in tide pools. They eat very tiny fish. Anemones are fun to spot. They look a bit like flowers.   They add a lot of color to a tide pool.

NAME:_____ DATE:_____

DIRECTIONS Read "Investigating Tide Pools" and then answer the questions.

1. Which shows a connection to the text?

Ⓐ I like to play in the sandbox at the park.

Ⓑ I play at the beach with my grandparents.

Ⓒ I noticed a tide pool on the beach and studied the creatures inside.

Ⓓ A starfish is a star.

2. What kind of bird likes to snack on mussels?

Ⓐ seagalls

Ⓑ seagulls

Ⓒ seagulps

Ⓓ seagails

3. When does the water leave the tide pool?

Ⓐ on a low ride

Ⓑ at low tide

Ⓒ on a low side

Ⓓ with a law ride

4. Why is a tide pool a unique habitat?

Ⓐ Starfish all look the same.

Ⓑ Birds prey on the food there.

Ⓒ It exists in low and high tides.

Ⓓ It is found on the beach.

5. Which is the best summary of the text?

Ⓐ Tide pools are unique habitats with interesting plants and animals.

Ⓑ Starfish like to eat mussels.

Ⓒ Tide pools take up space on our beaches.

Ⓓ Anemones eat tiny fish.

1. ☺ ☺
2. ☺ ☺
3. ☺ ☺
4. ☺ ☺
5. ☺ ☺

___ / 5
Total

NAME:_____ DATE:_____

SCORE
___/4

 Reread the text "Investigating Tide Pools."

 Think about what you would want to see on a trip to the beach.

Write about which creatures you would look for when you walk along the sand.

_____

_____

_____

_____

_____

_____

_____

_____

_____

_____

_____

NAME:_____ **DATE:**_____

DIRECTIONS Read the text and then answer the questions.

Felix has a special collection. He adds many items. They go into a nature box. He finds things on walks. Items catch his eye. Some days, he sees a rock. Other times, he finds a stick. He sees pretty flowers. Felix is proud of his collection.

1. ☺ ☹

2. ☺ ☹

1. Where does Felix find items for his nature box?

Ⓐ in a box

Ⓑ outside on his walks

Ⓒ at home

Ⓓ at school

3. What is the root word in *collection*?

Ⓐ lection

Ⓑ collect

Ⓒ coll

Ⓓ lect

3. ☺ ☹

4. ☺ ☹

____ / 4
Total

2. What is the main topic?

Ⓐ eyes

Ⓑ a collection

Ⓒ walking

Ⓓ flowers

4. What does the phrase *catch his eye* mean in the text?

Ⓐ get his attention

Ⓑ poke him in the eye

Ⓒ look at him

Ⓓ sparkle in the sun

NAME:_____ DATE:_____

SCORE

1. ☺ ☺

2. ☺ ☺

3. ☺ ☺

4. ☺ ☺

___/ 4
Total

DIRECTIONS Read the text and then answer the questions.

My teacher said that math is all around us. I was not sure what she meant. She told us to think about how we sort toys at home. We had to put them into different categories. My mom helped me. We sorted all my things into groups. I made a special chart that showed the groups. My teacher really liked my work.

1. Who is the narrator of the text?

(A) a student

(B) a teacher

(C) a principal

(D) a mom

2. Which title might best describe the main idea?

(A) A Teacher's Words

(B) Fun with Toys

(C) Math in the Real World

(D) Categories at Home

3. What is the root word in *showed*?

(A) show

(B) how

(C) howed

(D) owe

4. What did the teacher mean when she said math is *all around us*?

(A) Math time goes on all day.

(B) Math homework is never done.

(C) Math is about what is in the air.

(D) Math is found everywhere in the real world.

NAME:_____ **DATE:**_____

SCORE

1. ☺ ☹

2. ☺ ☹

3. ☺ ☹

4. ☺ ☹

____ / 4

Total

DIRECTIONS Read the text and then answer the questions.

Max loves his toy cars. Some days, he plays with them for hours. He has all different kinds of cars. Some of them are race cars, and others are trucks. He has a lot of different games he plays with them. His friends like cars too, so they trade cars with each other. Max prefers his cars to any other toy in the house.

1. What does Max like to play with more than his toy cars?

A clocks

B trucks

C games

D nothing

2. What is the main idea?

A Max has friends.

B Max likes race cars.

C Max enjoys his toy cars more than any other toy.

D Max trades cars.

3. Which word has the same root word as *preferred*?

A preformed

B preference

C referred

D referee

4. Which of these words means *preferred*?

A asked

B favored

C chose

D decided

NAME:_____ **DATE:**_____

Things that Come in Groups

Chloe is curious about something. She wonders what objects she can find at home that come in groups. First, she thinks about groups of two. What comes in groups of two?

Chloe goes into her closet first. Shoes and socks come in twos, and mittens and earmuffs do, too.

Chloe visits her kitchen. The salt and pepper shakers come in twos. A fork and a knife on the table come in twos. She notices the toaster and sees that it has two slots. That works in this group, too. Chloe's mom gives her an idea. Look in the mirror! There are other things that come in twos.

That reminds Chloe of something. Fingers and toes come in groups of five. They can also make groups of ten!

What about groups of twelve? Chloe counts eggs, her muffin tin, and her horse collection. All of those things come in groups of twelve.

Her mom has a question. She asks Chloe why she cares about groups. Chloe says, "I like it when things are not alone because a group is like a family." Her mom likes the kind thoughts behind Chloe's answer.

 #50923—180 Days of Reading for Second Grade

NAME:_____ **DATE:**_____

DIRECTIONS Read "Things that Come in Groups" and then answer the questions.

1. Which shows a connection to the text?

(A) I have a sticker collection.

(B) My eggs come in groups of 12, too.

(C) I have no socks on today.

(D) My closet is probably smaller than Chloe's closet.

2. Which group do mittens belong to?

(A) groups of two

(B) groups of too

(C) groups of tow

(D) groups of twee

3. What does the toaster have?

(A) two slots

(B) two slats

(C) two slits

(D) two salts

4. Which question did Chloe answer?

(A) What is 5 + 5?

(B) What objects at home come in groups?

(C) Where are my mittens?

(D) Why do eggs come in a carton?

5. Which would **not** belong in the text "Things that Come in Groups"?

(A) earrings

(B) thumbs

(C) flip-flops

(D) belly buttons

1. ☺ ☺

2. ☺ ☺

3. ☺ ☺

4. ☺ ☺

5. ☺ ☺

___ / 5
Total

NAME: _____ DATE: _____

 Reread the text "Things that Come in Groups."

 Think about the groups that exist in your home.

Write about and describe the groups and which categories they belong to.

_____

_____

_____

_____

_____

_____

_____

_____

_____

_____

_____

_____

_____

NAME:_____   **DATE:**_____

DIRECTIONS   Read the text and then answer the questions.

People live in small and large places. Smaller areas are called *towns*. Larger areas are called *cities*. These are grouped in one large space. This is called a *state*. Many states make a *country*. The people in one country are all different. But they have some things in common, too.

1. ☺ 😐

2. ☺ 😐

3. ☺ 😐

4. ☺ 😐

___ / 4
Total

1. What is the main idea?

(A) States are made up of cities and towns, and countries are made up of states.

(B) A state is larger than a town.

(C) Towns and cities are different.

(D) People in a country are not the same.

2. What is the difference between towns and cities?

(A) States are made up of cities, not towns.

(B) People live farther from each other in a town.

(C) Towns are in the country.

(D) Towns are smaller than cities.

3. What is the root word in *grouped*?

(A) gro

(B) group

(C) uped

(D) rouped

4. Which definition of *space* is used in this text?

(A) blank between words

(B) galaxy

(C) area

(D) room

NAME:_____ DATE:_____

DIRECTIONS Read the text and then answer the questions.

1. ☺ ☺

2. ☺ ☺

3. ☺ ☺

4. ☺ ☺

____ / 4
Total

> There are many different kinds of flags. They are usually in the shape of a rectangle. A flag can be held, or it can be flown. Some flags are even twirled! Flags wave in the wind. They have all sorts of designs on them. People hang flags to show respect. They may want to honor a special day.

1. Which title best fits the text?

(A) Flag Time

(B) Show Respect

(C) Flags for All Reasons

(D) Twirling

2. According to this text, how are flags used?

(A) They are held.

(B) They are flown.

(C) They are twirled.

(D) all of the above

3. How many syllables are in the word *designs*?

(A) one syllable

(B) two syllables

(C) three syllables

(D) four syllables

4. What else is in the shape of a *rectangle*?

(A) a door

(B) a clock

(C) a pizza slice

(D) a cupcake

 #50923—180 Days of Reading for Second Grade

NAME: _____ **DATE:** _____

DIRECTIONS Read the text and then answer the questions.

> The Olympic Games are a sporting event. They happen every two years. Athletes compete from around the world. They compete for medals. There are summer games. There are winter games. The athletes are the best in their sport. People all over the world like to watch. They root for their country!

1. ☺ 😐

2. ☺ 😐

3. ☺ 😐

4. ☺ 😐

___ / 4
Total

1. What is the main topic?

(A) sports

(B) the Olympic Games

(C) athletes

(D) summer and winter games

2. Which does **not** describe the Olympic Games?

(A) a sporting event in summer and winter

(B) a sporting event with countries competing against one another

(C) a sporting event that no one watches

(D) a sporting event with medals for the winners

3. Which word has the same root word as *sporting*?

(A) snorting

(B) sports

(C) chatting

(D) port

4. Which word means *to try to win*?

(A) watch

(B) root

(C) compete

(D) athletes

NAME:_____ DATE:_____

Symbols of a Country

People feel pride for a country. They share that pride with others. It makes a nation special.

Symbols show pride. They stand for a country. One type of symbol is a flag. Each flag is unique. People wave the flag. It shows respect. Flags are treated with honor.

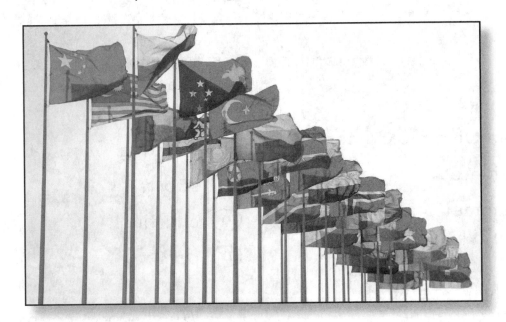

Countries have anthems. An *anthem* is a song. People learn the words. Anthems are sung at special times. They show support for a country. There are other special songs about countries, too. They are *patriotic* songs. People like to sing these songs. This means they are loyal.

People love their country. They want to visit special sites. These sites are part of a nation's history. A site might be a statue. Or it could be a monument. These are national treasures. They help people know about where they come from.

Each nation is unique. People feel pride for their homeland.

 #50923—*180 Days of Reading for Second Grade*

NAME:_____ DATE:_____

DIRECTIONS Read "Symbols of a Country" and then answer the questions.

1. Who might easily make a connection to the text?

(A) a person who loves to sing

(B) a student who says the Pledge of Allegiance each day

(C) a lifeguard who waves flags on the beach

(D) a person who enjoys road trips

2. What is an anthem?

(A) a song

(B) a sung

(C) a sang

(D) a singe

3. What is an example of a country's symbol?

(A) a falg

(B) a flig

(C) a flag

(D) a few

4. According to this text, how do people feel about their country?

(A) supportive

(B) scared

(C) full of pride

(D) confused

5. Which gives the best summary of the text?

(A) An anthem is a patriotic song.

(B) A flag is a symbol.

(C) A country's symbols are used to show pride and loyalty.

(D) A monument is a special site.

1. ☺ ☺

2. ☺ ☺

3. ☺ ☺

4. ☺ ☺

5. ☺ ☺

___ / 5
Total

NAME:_____ DATE:_____

 Reread the text "Symbols of a Country."

 Think about symbols of your home country.

Write about the symbols that are important to you. Why are they important to you?

_____

_____

_____

_____

_____

_____

_____

_____

_____

_____

_____

NAME:_____ **DATE:**_____

DIRECTIONS Read the text and then answer the questions.

The young girl walked on the beach. What did she see in the water? Was it a dolphin, a shark, or a whale? She knew something was out there. It had an interesting fin. She kept her eye on the same spot. Then, from the water emerged the head of a beautiful girl. She realized something amazing. She had just seen a mermaid.

1. ☺ ☺

2. ☺ ☺

3. ☺ ☺

4. ☺ ☺

____/4
Total

1. What happens right after the girl saw the fin?

Ⓐ She knew it was a mermaid.

Ⓑ She saw a head.

Ⓒ She kept her eye on the same spot.

Ⓓ She screamed.

2. How do you know the text is fantasy?

Ⓐ Young girls don't walk on the beach alone.

Ⓑ Mermaids are not real.

Ⓒ Mermaids are not girls.

Ⓓ Sharks and whales eat mermaids.

3. How many syllables are in the word *amazing*?

Ⓐ one syllable

Ⓑ two syllables

Ⓒ three syllables

Ⓓ four syllables

4. Which word means *realized*?

Ⓐ mentioned

Ⓑ found

Ⓒ breathed

Ⓓ understood

NAME:_____ DATE:_____

DIRECTIONS Read the text and then answer the questions.

Mom and Dad did not seem normal today. Our routine was different. They both got ready for work while I ate breakfast. They seemed a bit anxious about walking out the door. I got ready to walk to the bus stop. I looked for Dad to walk with me. That is when I noticed the odd object on our lawn. Why were Mom and Dad going inside it?

1. Who is the narrator of the text?

(A) a child

(B) a mother

(C) a father

(D) a Martian

2. Which title best fits the text?

(A) The Bus Stop

(B) A Normal Day

(C) A Strange Morning

(D) Breakfast with the Family

3. Which word has the same root word as *walking*?

(A) walked

(B) wall

(C) talking

(D) king

4. Which word does **not** give the reader a clue about the tone of the text?

(A) different

(B) ready

(C) anxious

(D) odd

NAME:_____ DATE:_____

DIRECTIONS Read the text and then answer the questions.

Jesse walked down the street and kept his eyes on the ground. "What are you doing, Jesse?" his mom asked. She was perplexed. Jesse kept hopping over something.

"I'm trying to avoid the cracks, Mom," said Jesse. Jesse was trying not to step on each crack in the sidewalk, and it was hard work. He thought something bad might happen if he stepped on a crack. He was being superstitious.

1. ☺ ☺

2. ☺ ☺

3. ☺ ☺

4. ☺ ☺

___/4
Total

1. Why is Jesse keeping his eyes on the ground?

(A) He does not want to talk to his mom.

(B) He is looking for cracks in the sidewalk.

(C) He is looking for insects to step on.

(D) He is trying to be good.

2. Why is Jesse avoiding sidewalk cracks?

(A) He thinks something bad might happen.

(B) He likes to hop.

(C) He is frustrated with his mom.

(D) He cannot see them.

3. Which root word with an –ed ending is **not** in the text?

(A) walk

(B) perplex

(C) step

(D) work

4. What is an example of being *superstitious*?

(A) wearing a bicycle helmet

(B) not ever choosing unlucky number 13

(C) not watching television for a week

(D) walking backwards out of a room

NAME:_____ DATE:_____

A Magical Surprise

Nate loved his new magic set. He practiced his tricks every day, he knew all the words to say, and he knew how to use his props. He wanted to put on a special magic show.

Nate decided to invite all his friends and family to his show. On the day of the show, people came over to his house. When everyone sat down, Nate started the show. He did three tricks. Each trick went well. The audience was enjoying his magic. Then he took out his final trick. He hid a stuffed rabbit in a big, black hat. When he said the magic words, the rabbit was supposed to come back. He had practiced the trick many times. But this time, it did not work. Kids in the audience started to laugh. Nate was mortified.

Nate held his wand tight. He closed his eyes. He made a wish. He said, "I wish this magic show would disappear." He said the magic word, and then he opened his eyes. The room was empty! His wand was magical. It granted Nate his wish.

Nate was not sure what to do next. Should he tell his parents? Should he wish for a million dollars? Instead he began to worry. He thought about what might have happened to his friends. He was scared for them. So Nate closed his eyes. He used his wand again. When he opened his eyes, the audience was waiting for him. It was like they had never been gone. Nate finished his final trick and took a bow. The audience clapped loudly. His first show was a success. Had Nate really made the audience disappear, or did he just think he did? Nate won't ever tell. A magician never reveals his secrets!

NAME:_____ DATE:_____

DIRECTIONS Read "A Magical Surprise" and then answer the questions.

1. Which shows a connection to this text?

Ⓐ I make posters for a lot of events.

Ⓑ I do not know many of my neighbors.

Ⓒ I like to imagine that I have secret magical powers, too.

Ⓓ I think a magic wand is dangerous.

2. What did Nate practice?

Ⓐ a trip

Ⓑ a trim

Ⓒ a train

Ⓓ a trick

3. What did Nate make using his wand?

Ⓐ a wind

Ⓑ a dish

Ⓒ a wish

Ⓓ a swish

4. How does Nate respond to learning about the magic of his wand?

Ⓐ He went to his brother for help.

Ⓑ He decided to no longer do any magic.

Ⓒ He thought of everything he could wish for.

Ⓓ He was worried about people being hurt by his magic.

5. Which gives the best summary of the text?

Ⓐ Nate was surprised by the magic that was created at his own magic show.

Ⓑ Nate got a new magic set.

Ⓒ Nate did four tricks at a magic show.

Ⓓ Nate made posters for his neighbors.

1. ☺ ☺

2. ☺ ☺

3. ☺ ☺

4. ☺ ☺

5. ☺ ☺

____ / 5
Total

SCORE

___ / 4

NAME:_____ **DATE:**_____

 Reread the text "A Magical Surprise."

 Think about how Nate reacted to having a magic wand.

Write about what you would do with a magic wand.

_____

_____

_____

_____

_____

_____

_____

_____

_____

_____

_____

_____

NAME:_____ **DATE:**_____

DIRECTIONS Read the text and then answer the questions.

Dinosaurs used to roam Earth. Now they are gone. We do not know for sure where they went or what happened to them. Scientists have theories. Some say an asteroid hit Earth, while others think a disease spread among the dinosaurs. An ice age may have started it all. We may never know the real truth.

1. 😊 😐

2. 😊 😐

3. 😊 😐

4. 😊 😐

___/4
Total

1. What is the main idea of this text?

(A) Scientists develop theories.

(B) The reason why dinosaurs are gone is a mystery.

(C) Asteroids hit Earth.

(D) An ice age may have happened.

2. Which idea is **not** suggested as a reason why dinosaurs are gone?

(A) disease

(B) asteroids

(C) an ice age

(D) a volcano eruption

3. What is the root word in *started*?

(A) tart

(B) start

(C) ted

(D) art

4. Which word is a synonym for *roam*?

(A) destroy

(B) attack

(C) rule

(D) travel

NAME:_____ **DATE:**_____

SCORE

1. ☺ ☹

2. ☺ ☹

3. ☺ ☹

4. ☺ ☹

___/ 4
Total

DIRECTIONS Read the text and then answer the questions.

Sea turtles are amazing. They can swim a long way. They can swim over 1,000 miles! But sea turtles are in trouble. Their numbers are low. Nests are disturbed by humans. Eggs are often taken. Babies cannot survive. This is a big problem.

1. Which title best fits the text?

(A) Nest Disturbance

(B) A Long Swim

(C) Sea Turtles in Danger

(D) All About Baby Turtles

2. What is the problem?

(A) Sea turtles swim a long way.

(B) Sea turtles' nests and eggs are disturbed.

(C) Sea turtles cross oceans.

(D) Sea turtles are amazing.

3. How many syllables are in the word *survive*?

(A) one syllable

(B) two syllables

(C) three syllables

(D) four syllables

4. What does the phrase *numbers are low* mean in the text above?

(A) Sea turtles are swimming lower.

(B) The number of sea turtles is shrinking.

(C) Sea turtles are getting smaller.

(D) Sea turtles are eating less.

NAME:_____ DATE:_____

DIRECTIONS Read the text and then answer the questions.

Plants can become extinct. When they are extinct, they are gone forever. One fewer species might not seem like a big deal. There are many others left. Yet plants are vital to life. We need plants to stay alive. Other living things depend on plants, too.

1. ☺ ☹

2. ☺ ☹

3. ☺ ☹

4. ☺ ☹

___ / 4
Total

1. What is the main idea?

(A) extinct animals

(B) extinct plants

(C) plant species

(D) living things

2. People should worry about plants becoming extinct because

(A) we would have no dirt.

(B) they are more important than extinct animals.

(C) we need plants to survive.

(D) plants are pretty to look at.

3. Which word has the same root word as *living*?

(A) having

(B) lived

(C) loving

(D) olive

4. Which words are synonyms?

(A) *plant* and *things*

(B) *animal* and *vital*

(C) *alive* and *living*

(D) *extinct* and *less*

Ecosystems

Our world has many creatures. We all depend on one another. We need one another to survive. One creature may die out. That changes the rest of the living world.

Many fish are close to extinction. Imagine a lake full of fish. Humans have hunted them. We wanted them for food. We fished for them. We kept fishing for them. Over time, there were fewer fish.

But the fish are part of a large ecosystem. They eat tadpoles. They eat insects. With fewer fish, there are now more insects. There are many more frogs. The frogs need more food. Frogs eat dragonflies. But now they have eaten too many dragonflies.

One lake has been overfished. The ecosystem has changed.

Humans caused this problem. The fish are almost extinct. What can humans do now? How can we fix the problem?

Some people may suggest closing the lake. Perhaps there will be no fishing there for several years. This would give the fish time to come back. It would help restore the balance of life in that lake.

These kinds of problems are happening in many places. Many animals face this kind of issue. Humans are often the problem. But they can be the solution, too.

NAME:_____ **DATE:**_____

DIRECTIONS Read "Ecosystems" and then answer the questions.

1. Which experience would help you understand the text?

(A) Yesterday, I noticed there were not many birds by my house and there have been a lot of insects around lately.

(B) I have tasted fish before and I don't like it.

(C) My sister and I swim in the lake on the weekends.

(D) The local pond is closed for the winter because the water is too cold.

2. What is the text about?

(A) a lock

(B) a leek

(C) a luck

(D) a lake

3. What animal is described in the text?

(A) a fish

(B) a dish

(C) a flash

(D) a fit

4. What is the problem?

(A) hungry frogs

(B) a destroyed ecosystem

(C) a lack of fish for fishermen

(D) a cold lake

5. Which best summarizes the text?

(A) All living creatures eat tadpoles.

(B) Living creatures depend on one another for a healthy ecosystem.

(C) All living creatures need clean lakes as a habitat.

(D) A lake needs more fish.

1. ☺ ☺
2. ☺ ☺
3. ☺ ☺
4. ☺ ☺
5. ☺ ☺

___ / 5
Total

NAME: _____ **DATE:** _____

 Reread the text "Ecosystems."

 Think about how everything that is alive is connected.

Write about what this reminds you of in your own life.

_____

_____

_____

_____

_____

_____

_____

_____

_____

_____

_____

NAME:_____ **DATE:**_____

DIRECTIONS   Read the text and then answer the questions.

> Luis wanted to go camping. His mom said no. His dad said no, too. But Luis could not give up on his idea. His parents said they were too busy. Camping took a lot of time to plan. It was a long drive to the lake. Wait! Luis had an idea. He got the tent. He set it up in the yard. He ate hot dogs and s'mores with his family. It was the best camping trip ever!

1. ☺ ☺

2. ☺ ☺

3. ☺ ☺

4. ☺ ☺

____ / 4

Total

1. What problem does Luis solve?

(A) His brother was too scared to sleep outside.

(B) His parents didn't want to plan a camping trip.

(C) His dad lost the tent.

(D) His mom did not know how to cook a hot dog.

2. What is Luis's idea?

(A) He decides to put up a tent in the yard.

(B) He asks his mom and dad to go camping.

(C) He gets marshmallows for s'mores.

(D) He goes to sleep in the tent.

3. What is the root word in *camping*?

(A) camping

(B) camp

(C) –ing

(D) camper

4. Which of these words means *idea*?

(A) busy

(B) good

(C) thought

(D) route

NAME:_____ **DATE:**_____

DIRECTIONS Read the text and then answer the questions.

1. ☺☹

    Cassie and Lily had a pillow fight. They were giggling. One of the pillows ripped. Feathers were everywhere! It was raining feathers! Cassie's mom heard the ruckus. She took one look in Cassie's room. She laughed. The girls helped her clean up the feathers.

2. ☺☹

3. ☺☹

1. What does the text tell you about Cassie and Lily's friendship?

- (A) They always make a mess.
- (B) They like to have fun.
- (C) They argue over toys.
- (D) They do not like to clean up.

4. ☺☹

____/ 4
Total

2. Which title best fits the text?

- (A) Playdate Fun
- (B) Itchy Feathers
- (C) Pillows Are for Sleeping
- (D) Cassie's Room

3. Which suffix could be added to *rain* to make a new word?

- (A) –ed
- (B) –ly
- (C) –tion
- (D) –er

4. What does it mean when the author says it was *raining feathers*?

- (A) The feathers got wet.
- (B) The feathers came from the pillow.
- (C) The feathers fell from above like rain.
- (D) The feathers made everyone sneeze.

NAME:_____ **DATE:**_____

DIRECTIONS   Read the text and then answer the questions.

SCORE

1. ☺ 😐

2. ☺ 😐

3. ☺ 😐

4. ☺ 😐

_____ / 4
Total

The two sisters had worked out a plan for nighttime, when their parents were asleep. They had to stay quiet so that no one would know they were staying up late. The two girls used flashlights to send signals to each other. They had agreed on a code. They felt like secret spies! It was a lot of fun. This was why they never wanted to go to sleep.

1. Why do the two sisters use the flashlights?

(A) to read books at night

(B) to send messages to each other

(C) to see the way to the bathroom

(D) to make things look spooky

2. Which adjective best describes what the girls do at night?

(A) useful

(B) spoiled

(C) sneaky

(D) fast

3. Which word has the same root word as *staying*?

(A) saying

(B) stayed

(C) starving

(D) starry

4. Which is another example of a *code*?

(A) a computer password

(B) a cell phone

(C) a board game

(D) a baseball bat

The Fort

Max knew that a fort would be easy to make. First he found some pillows. Then he got a blanket from his bed. He picked a spot near the couch to build his fort. It was wobbly, but it still stood up.

The fort became his calm spot that he liked to go into every day. He put his toys in there, including his new robot. That took up a lot of room, but he didn't care.

When Sam came over for a visit, the two boys added on to the fort. They wanted to have room for both of them, but they did not always agree on how to build the fort. Sometimes, Max wanted things to be a certain way. Sam would get angry, and the two friends would argue about it. But they always found a way to work it out.

One day, Max's little sister, Grace, wanted to come into his fort. He yelled at her to get out. His mom was really upset. "Max, you can't keep your sister out because this room is her space, too," said his mom. Max felt frustrated because it was his only quiet space in the whole house. For a long time, he thought about how to solve his problem.

"Grace, do you want your own fort? I will help you make one," Max told his sister. Grace was thrilled. The two kids spent the morning getting it all ready. They worked together. Now there were two great forts in the house!

NAME:_____ **DATE:**_____

DIRECTIONS Read "The Fort" and then answer the questions.

1. Who might make a connection to the text?

(A) a girl who argues with her teacher

(B) a mother who does not like forts

(C) a boy who does not like to share with his sister

(D) a babysitter who gets mad when siblings fight

2. What spot does Max pick to build his fort?

(A) near the coach

(B) near the crouch

(C) near the couch

(D) near the cowch

3. Sam and Max _____ about the fort.

(A) angry

(B) are

(C) added

(D) argued

4. Max's mother says that this was Grace's space, too, because

(A) Grace does not like forts.

(B) the fort is built in a place where Grace is allowed to go.

(C) Grace and Max share a bedroom.

(D) Grace watches television on the couch.

5. What clue helps you understand that Max will solve the problem with Grace?

(A) Max likes to be in his fort by himself.

(B) Max gets frustrated by his wobbly fort.

(C) Max's mother is upset with him and his angry tone.

(D) Max solves problems well with Sam.

1. ☺ ☹

2. ☺ ☹

3. ☺ ☹

4. ☺ ☹

5. ☺ ☹

___ / 5
Total

NAME:_____ **DATE:**_____

Reread the text "The Fort."

Think about a time when you wanted to be alone and not share space with anyone else.

Write about making a quiet place for yourself. How does being alone help you?

_____

_____

_____

_____

_____

_____

_____

_____

_____

_____

#50923—180 Days of Reading for Second Grade   © Shell Education

NAME:_____ DATE:_____

DIRECTIONS Read the text and then answer the questions.

    A snowy owl is a beautiful creature. The name of the owl is a good one because the owl is as white as snow. A male snowy owl grows whiter with age. The females have more dark spots. Snowy owls wait for prey. They have a keen sense of hearing that helps them catch their next meal.

1. 🙂 😐

2. 🙂 😐

3. 🙂 😐

4. 🙂 😐

1. What is the text mostly about?

(A) snowy owls

(B) an owl's diet

(C) snow

(D) an owl's sense of hearing

____ / 4

Total

2. Why does a snowy owl's name make sense?

(A) They fly south, away from the snow.

(B) They live in the snow.

(C) They are as white as snow.

(D) They eat snow.

3. What is the root word in *beautiful*?

(A) tiful

(B) beauty

(C) beau

(D) ful

4. What does the word *prey* mean?

(A) nocturnal animals

(B) smart animals

(C) meat eaters

(D) animals hunted by other animals

NAME:_____ DATE:_____

DIRECTIONS Read the text and then answer the questions.

> The moon is always orbiting around Earth. The moon goes through cycles, which means that our view of the moon is changing even though a whole moon is always in space. Some nights, we see a full moon. Other nights, it is a half-moon. A quarter-moon looks like a skinny sliver. On some nights, we see no moon at all! This is called a *new moon*.

1. Which title best fits the text?

(A) Things That Orbit

(B) A Changing, Orbiting Moon

(C) Half Moons

(D) New Moons Are No Moons

2. What does *the cycles of the moon* mean?

(A) We only see a full moon in the summer.

(B) Our view changes as the moon orbits Earth.

(C) We see a different moon than others.

(D) The moon changes over time.

3. How many syllables are in the word *orbiting*?

(A) one syllable

(B) two syllables

(C) three syllables

(D) four syllables

4. When might you use the word *half* to describe something?

(A) when reading a recipe

(B) when discussing the hoof of a horse

(C) when talking about something you own

(D) when describing the playground at school

NAME:_____ DATE:_____

Read the text and then answer the questions.

The night sky is beautiful to watch. There are millions of stars. Some stars form pictures. People have named those pictures. They are called *constellations*. They make stargazing fun!

1. ☺ 😐

2. ☺ 😐

3. ☺ 😐

1. What is the main idea?

(A) Shooting stars are rare.

(B) It is fun to look for constellations in the night sky.

(C) There are millions of stars to see.

(D) Constellations are weird pictures.

2. Why is the night sky beautiful to watch?

(A) because stars are so far away

(B) because you never know what you will find

(C) because stars twinkle

(D) because you can see constellations

3. Which word has the same root word as *named*?

(A) nominee

(B) tamed

(C) rename

(D) medicine

4. What are *constellations*?

(A) the night sky

(B) the moon

(C) stars that form pictures

(D) stargazing

4. ☺ 😐

___ / 4
Total

NAME:_____ DATE:_____

What Comes Alive at Night?

It's the middle of the night. Most people are home in bed. A whole other world comes alive at night. These creatures are alert. They are *nocturnal*. They stay awake at night and sleep during the day.

Nocturnal animals have ways to survive at night. They must find food. They also have to escape predators. Nocturnal animals may have a strong sense of sight. This helps them see things in the dark. Many nocturnal animals also smell quite well. They can smell food. They can also sense danger.

A cat is a nocturnal animal. Cats can see well in the darkness. This helps them spot food. They have excellent hearing, too. They can even hear the high-pitched sounds mice make. Humans cannot hear these pitches.

An owl is also nocturnal. It has strong hearing and vision, too. This helps an owl swoop down on its prey. Owls, like cats, are good hunters.

NAME:_____ **DATE:**_____

DIRECTIONS Read "What Comes Alive at Night?" and then answer the questions.

1. Which shows a connection to the text?

(A) My dog likes to go to the dog park.

(B) I had an interesting dream last night.

(C) I have a cat that likes to explore at night.

(D) I get scared by the dark.

2. What can cats hear?

(A) a high pits

(B) a high pitch

(C) a high stitch

(D) a high pit

3. Where are most people at night?

(A) in bed

(B) in bid

(C) in bad

(D) in bud

4. Which statement about owls and cats is true?

(A) Owls and cats are good hunters.

(B) Owls and cats are nocturnal.

(C) Owls and cats have strong hearing and vision.

(D) all of the above

5. Which summary best describes the text?

(A) Nocturnal animals can only survive at nighttime.

(B) Owls are nocturnal. They are good at hunting at night.

(C) Nocturnal animals are awake at night and sleep during the day. They have strong senses to help them hunt.

(D) Owls and cats hunt at night. This means they are nocturnal.

1. ☺ ☺

2. ☺ ☺

3. ☺ ☺

4. ☺ ☺

5. ☺ ☺

_____ / 5

Total

NAME: _____ DATE: _____

 Reread the text "What Comes Alive at Night?"

 Think about how different creatures are awake at night while you sleep.

 Write about a time when you noticed a nocturnal animal. What did the animal look like? What was it doing?

_____

_____

_____

_____

_____

_____

_____

_____

_____

_____

NAME:_____ **DATE:**_____

Read the text and then answer the questions.

Kevin did not want to take lessons at the pool. "I know how to swim," he insisted.

"You have to be really safe in the water," his dad said.

Kevin thought swim lessons would take the fun out of it. He liked to be wild in the pool. His dad wanted him to know that it was important to be safe while swimming.

1. ☺ ☺

2. ☺ ☺

3. ☺ ☺

4. ☺ ☺

1. What does Kevin's dad say about swimming?

(A) Kevin should be wild in the pool.

(B) Kevin does not need lessons.

(C) Kevin has to be safe in the water.

(D) Lessons will take the fun out of swimming.

2. What is the text mostly about?

(A) being wild

(B) Kevin's dad

(C) swim lessons

(D) swimming pools

3. What is the root word in *wanted*?

(A) ted

(B) ant

(C) anted

(D) want

4. What does the phrase *take the fun out of it* mean in the text?

(A) make something safe

(B) make something less fun

(C) make something more fun

(D) make something dangerous

____ / 4
Total

NAME:_____ DATE:_____

SCORE

1. ☺ ☹

2. ☺ ☹

3. ☺ ☹

4. ☺ ☹

_____ / 4
Total

DIRECTIONS Read the text and then answer the questions.

> Owen had to get stitches. He had been climbing a tree. He stepped up to a branch but fell to the ground. On his way down, he hit the side of his head. Owen thought it was fine, but his mom was concerned. She wanted the doctor to examine Owen's head. The doctor knew right away that Owen needed stitches.

1. What happens right after Owen steps up to a branch?

(A) He cried out for his mom.

(B) He hit his head and fell to the ground.

(C) He had to get stitches.

(D) He went to the doctor.

2. What is the text mostly about?

(A) why Owen had to get stitches

(B) where Owen had to get stitches

(C) how many stitches Owen had to get

(D) how Owen felt about getting stitches

3. How many syllables are in the word *concerned*?

(A) one syllable

(B) two syllables

(C) three syllables

(D) four syllables

4. What does it mean for the doctor to *examine* Owen's head?

(A) feel

(B) bandage

(C) measure

(D) look closely at

NAME: _____ **DATE:** _____

DIRECTIONS Read the text and then answer the questions.

Marla was excited about her trip. She was going on an airplane! She was visiting her family. Marla told her friend Beth about the trip. Beth asked Marla when she was leaving, because Beth's birthday party was soon. Oh no! Marla was going to miss Beth's party. How sad!

1. ☺ ☺

2. ☺ ☺

3. ☺ ☺

4. ☺ ☺

1. What is the problem?

Ⓐ Marla will miss her friend's party when she is on her trip.

Ⓑ Marla and Beth are not friends.

Ⓒ Beth is having a party.

Ⓓ Marla is going on an airplane.

2. What is the main idea?

Ⓐ Marla going on an airplane

Ⓑ Beth's party

Ⓒ Marla's trip and its bad timing

Ⓓ Marla's family visit

3. Which word is a compound word?

Ⓐ excited

Ⓑ airplane

Ⓒ leaving

Ⓓ going

4. What does *miss* mean in this text?

Ⓐ unable to attend something

Ⓑ not hit a target

Ⓒ avoid something

Ⓓ forget something

_____ / 4
Total

NAME: _____ DATE: _____

No Swimming this Summer

Breaking an arm is never good news. Anna knew this now for sure. She broke her arm on Saturday. She was climbing a ladder at the park. Anna loved to climb. She wanted to go down the slide. But she fell to the ground. When she landed, her arm hurt terribly. Anna's mother knew something was wrong, so they went to the doctor right away. The doctor took an X-ray with a special camera. The pictures showed Anna's bones. It was clear that one of her bones was broken.

Anna was sad. She would have a cast on her arm for six weeks. She could not write or play catch. Worst of all, she could not go swimming.

It was summertime, and Anna loved to swim each day. What would she do without her swim time? This was going to be the worst summer ever!

Anna's mom felt bad for Anna because she knew that being in a cast would be no fun. She knew how much Anna loved being in the water. She had an idea. Anna's mom got a special plastic bag. She wrapped it around Anna's cast. Anna could sit on the steps of the pool. As long as she kept her arm dry, she could play a bit in the water.

It was not perfect. Anna still could not swim, but now she could go in the water. She was grateful that her mom had helped her. Maybe this summer would not be so bad after all.

 #50923—180 Days of Reading for Second Grade

NAME:_____ DATE:_____

DIRECTIONS Read "No Swimming this Summer" and then answer the questions.

1. Which shows a connection to the text?

Ⓐ I like to play soccer.

Ⓑ I sprained my ankle and missed a dance recital.

Ⓒ I think bones are fragile.

Ⓓ I don't like how hot it gets in the summertime.

2. What does Anna have to get?

Ⓐ a cost

Ⓑ a crast

Ⓒ a cast

Ⓓ a chast

3. Anna's mom gets a special plastic bag to _____ around her arm.

Ⓐ rap

Ⓑ wrap

Ⓒ wrape

Ⓓ rope

4. What is the problem?

Ⓐ Anna's mom was nice to Anna.

Ⓑ Anna could not run fast.

Ⓒ The doctor saw Anna's broken arm.

Ⓓ Anna had a broken arm and could not enjoy the pool.

5. How does Anna feel by the end?

Ⓐ grateful and optimistic

Ⓑ angry

Ⓒ confused and sad

Ⓓ irritated

1. ☺ ☺

2. ☺ ☺

3. ☺ ☺

4. ☺ ☺

5. ☺ ☺

___/5
Total

SCORE

___/4

 Reread the text "No Swimming this Summer."

 Think about how Anna's plans for the summer had to change even though she did not want them to.

Write about a time when you had to change your plans. Why did you change them, and what happened instead?

_____

_____

_____

_____

_____

_____

_____

_____

_____

_____

_____

_____

_____

NAME:_____ DATE:_____

DIRECTIONS Read the text and then answer the questions.

A compass shows direction. It tells you where north, south, east, and west are. Compasses have been used for a long time. Ships used to rely on compasses. Compasses told them which way to travel. People still use compasses today. They are smaller. They are easier to use. Yet they are still the same tool found in history.

1. ☺ ☺

2. ☺ ☺

3. ☺ ☺

4. ☺ ☺

1. What is the main idea?

Ⓐ travel

Ⓑ direction

Ⓒ compasses

Ⓓ ships

2. Which idea is **not** suggested in this text?

Ⓐ A compass shows direction.

Ⓑ A compass is a globe.

Ⓒ A compass tells people which way to travel.

Ⓓ Compasses have been used for a long time.

3. Which word has the same root word as *smaller*?

Ⓐ smallest

Ⓑ mall

Ⓒ taller

Ⓓ smell

4. Which word in the text means *instrument*?

Ⓐ travel

Ⓑ tool

Ⓒ direction

Ⓓ time

____ / 4
Total

NAME:_____ **DATE:**_____

DIRECTIONS Read the text and then answer the questions.

A lake on a map should not look larger than an ocean! Drawing to *scale* is important. It means that objects are sized as they look next to other objects. Artists think about scale. So do architects. They draw designs to scale. Mapmakers work with scale, too.

1. Which title best captures the main idea?

(A) Lakes and Oceans

(B) Drawing to Scale

(C) A Mapmaker's Work

(D) An Artist's Skill

2. What is the text mostly about?

(A) maps

(B) scale

(C) architects

(D) artists

3. How many syllables are in the word *architect*?

(A) five syllables

(B) two syllables

(C) three syllables

(D) four syllables

4. Which definition of *scale* is used in this text?

(A) fish skin

(B) weighing machine

(C) climb

(D) correct size

NAME:_____ DATE:_____

DIRECTIONS Read the text and then answer the questions.

A globe is a model of Earth. It is in the shape of a sphere. Globes have to be updated. They have to show what the world looks like today. Countries' borders shift, and names can change. Sometimes, a lake or a river even disappears. The world never stays the same.

1. ☺ ☺

2. ☺ ☺

1. What is the main idea?

(A) A river can disappear.

(B) A globe is a model of Earth, which is always changing.

(C) A globe is a sphere.

(D) A globe changes.

3. ☺ ☺

4. ☺ ☺

_____ / 4
Total

3. Which word has the same root word as *updated*?

(A) ate

(B) dating

(C) upstairs

(D) dash

2. Why does a globe always have to change?

(A) because the borders of lakes change

(B) because borders disappear

(C) because maps are a lot of work

(D) because the world is changing

4. Which of these words have similar meanings?

(A) *updated* and *change*

(B) *shift* and *disappear*

(C) *shape* and *world*

(D) *model* and *sphere*

NAME:_____ DATE:_____

Parts of a Map

Maps show us information. A map is a visual picture that represents a place. Maps show locations to tell us more about them. They may tell us where to find city roads. They can show where a river flows. Maps can even show changes in the weather.

Maps show objects as symbols. For example, a road might be shown as a blue line on a map. A park might be shown as a tree. A school might be shown as a bell. These symbols are found in a key. The *key* tells what each symbol means. A key is also called a *legend*.

Maps also have a compass rose. This shows direction. The compass rose shows north and south. It shows east and west, too. People who use maps rely on the compass to show them direction. It reminds us where places are compared to other places.

A map has to be drawn to scale. A map of a country cannot be as big as a real country! A map drawn to scale is smaller than what it actually shows.

Maps tell us a lot about the world around us.

NAME:_____ **DATE:**_____

DIRECTIONS Read "Parts of a Map" and then answer the questions.

1. Who might easily make a connection to the text?

(A) a clockmaker

(B) an architect who draws to scale

(C) a person who is planning a road trip

(D) a person who weighs herself on a scale

2. Which tells what map symbols mean?

(A) a key

(B) a kay

(C) a koi

(D) a keep

3. A map is drawn to

(A) scar.

(B) seal.

(C) school.

(D) scale.

4. How do map symbols work?

(A) They need to be read carefully because they are hard to see.

(B) They are not important because you should know what is around you.

(C) They show where the key is.

(D) They show where places are.

5. Which is the best summary of the text?

(A) Maps must change.

(B) Maps show direction.

(C) Maps give information about the world around us.

(D) Maps are drawn to scale.

1. ☺ ☹
2. ☺ ☹
3. ☺ ☹
4. ☺ ☹
5. ☺ ☹

___ / 5
Total

NAME:_____ DATE:_____

 Reread the text "Parts of a Map."

 Think about some of the reasons why maps are useful.

✏️ **Write about** a time when you got to use a map. Was it helpful?

_____

_____

_____

_____

_____

_____

_____

_____

_____

_____

_____

NAME:_____ **DATE:**_____

DIRECTIONS Read the text and then answer the questions.

Hugo's family had a tradition. It was for New Year's Eve. They did the same thing every year. They made a video. In the video, they talked about the year. Hugo picked his best moments. So did his parents and his sister. They shared their wishes for the new year.

1. When does Hugo's family tradition take place?

(A) in the new year

(B) on New Year's Eve

(C) during the previous year

(D) on New Year's Day

2. What is the text mostly about?

(A) a holiday

(B) a family

(C) a video

(D) a family tradition

3. Which word from the text has three syllables?

(A) tradition

(B) talked

(C) moments

(D) wishes

4. Which is an example of a *tradition*?

(A) riding in the car

(B) eating candy

(C) having a family dinner every Sunday night

(D) eating pizza

SCORE

1. ☺ ☺

2. ☺ ☺

3. ☺ ☺

4. ☺ ☺

___ / 4
Total

NAME: _____ **DATE:** _____

DIRECTIONS Read the text and then answer the questions.

Jack wanted a pet dragon so badly. His mother told him that dragons were make-believe. His father also said that he could not buy a dragon. Jack did not care. He knew that there was a dragon out there. Jack had been reading about dragons. His dream was to have one of his very own.

1. What is Jack's problem?

Ⓐ Jack wants a pet dragon.

Ⓑ Jack wants a book about dragons.

Ⓒ Jack is angry with his parents.

Ⓓ Jack wants a pet.

2. Which title describes the main idea?

Ⓐ Arguing with Mom and Dad

Ⓑ No Pets Allowed

Ⓒ Wishing for a Dragon

Ⓓ Story Time

3. How many syllables are in the word *dragon*?

Ⓐ one syllable

Ⓑ two syllables

Ⓒ three syllables

Ⓓ four syllables

4. Which of the following is *make-believe*?

Ⓐ a dolphin

Ⓑ a unicorn

Ⓒ a skeleton

Ⓓ a puppy

#50923—180 Days of Reading for Second Grade

NAME:_____ **DATE:**_____

Read the text and then answer the questions.

SCORE

Angie wanted to play checkers, so she asked her sister, Nina, "Will you play checkers with me?"

Nina said, "Only if I can be red."

"But I want to be red," said Angie. The two girls could not agree. Both loved red. It was their favorite color. Finally, Angie had a compromise. Nina could be red first, then she would be red next. That idea worked!

1. ☺ ☹

2. ☺ ☹

3. ☺ ☹

4. ☺ ☹

____ / 4
Total

1. What is the problem?

Ⓐ Angie and Nina cannot decide what to play.

Ⓑ Nina won't let Angie borrow her red sweater.

Ⓒ Angie and Nina both want to use the red checkers.

Ⓓ There is no problem in the text.

2. What does the text tell you about compromising?

Ⓐ It happens when you play checkers.

Ⓑ It makes people angry.

Ⓒ It's about taking turns.

Ⓓ It never works.

3. Which word has the same root word as *worked*?

Ⓐ walked

Ⓑ worried

Ⓒ working

Ⓓ parked

4. Which of these words means *compromise*?

Ⓐ disagreement

Ⓑ agreement

Ⓒ argument

Ⓓ disappointment

NAME:_____ DATE:_____

Happy New Year!

My family celebrates the new year. We do not just do this once. We do this twice each year. How? We greet the new year on January 1st. Then, we have Chinese New Year. It is a different day each year. It follows the Chinese calendar. This calendar follows the moon. It is also called the *lunar calendar*.

Chinese New Year is a big deal. It lasts for 15 days. My entire family gets together. We have many traditions. We wear red. Red is a symbol for fire. It drives away bad luck. So do fireworks. We hear a lot of fireworks during this time. My family has a big feast, too. We usually eat fish. We also love dumplings.

The big finale is the Lantern Festival. It is the last night of the 15 days. People hang glowing lanterns. They carry them, too. There is often a dragon dance. A moving dragon is usually made of paper or silk. Young men hold the dragon. They guide it through the streets. This is my favorite night of the year!

NAME:_____ DATE:_____

Read "Happy New Year!" and then answer the questions.

SCORE

1. Who might make a connection to the text?

(A) an artist who makes lanterns

(B) a child who loves fireworks on July 4th

(C) a man who likes to wear red

(D) families who celebrate Hanukkah with many traditions

2. What color is good luck?

(A) rod

(B) rad

(C) red

(D) rid

3. What do people do during the Lantern Festival?

(A) hung lanterns

(B) hang lanterns

(C) bang lanterns

(D) rang lanterns

4. Which best summarizes the Lantern Festival?

(A) It lasts for 15 days. My family always makes sure to wear red.

(B) It is also called the *lunar calendar*.

(C) It occurs twice a year. We first celebrate it on January 1st.

(D) It happens on the last day of the Chinese New Year. People hang lanterns and watch a paper dragon move through the streets.

5. Which best summarizes the text?

(A) A family only wears red.

(B) A family's traditions for Chinese New Year are very special.

(C) The Lantern Festival is the last night of the New Year.

(D) A dragon dance moves through the street.

1. ☺ ☺

2. ☺ ☺

3. ☺ ☺

4. ☺ ☺

5. ☺ ☺

___ / 5

Total

NAME:_____ DATE:_____

SCORE

___ / 4

 Reread the text "Happy New Year!"

 Think about a holiday tradition that is important to you and your family.

Write about and describe your tradition. What makes your tradition special?

_____

_____

_____

_____

_____

_____

_____

_____

_____

_____

_____

NAME:_____ **DATE:**_____

DIRECTIONS   Read the text and then answer the questions.

Many kids want to be race car drivers. They like the idea of going fast. Cars are exciting and fun. Some kids get started on the hobby early. They build small go-karts. This can be a fun thing to do with a parent. It is really important to follow a good plan!

1. ☺ ☺

2. ☺ ☺

1. What is the text mostly about?

(A) following a plan

(B) working together with a parent

(C) cars and go-karts

(D) hobbies

3. What is the root word in *exciting*?

(A) excite

(B) exci

(C) ting

(D) citi

3. ☺ ☺

4. ☺ ☺

____ / 4
Total

2. What do kids do in order to follow their dreams of being race car drivers?

(A) They spend time with a parent.

(B) They run fast.

(C) They find a hobby.

(D) They build go-karts.

4. What is another word for the word *plan* in the last sentence?

(A) decision

(B) race track

(C) calendar

(D) drawing

NAME:_____ **DATE:**_____

DIRECTIONS Read the text and then answer the questions.

Track and field is a sport. It includes running, jumping, and throwing. Athletes compete in a stadium. There is a large oval track. Runners race around the track. Some races are long. The longest is over six miles. Other races are very short. They are called *sprints*.

1. Which title best fits the text?

Ⓐ Jumping for Sport

Ⓑ Around the Track

Ⓒ Facts About Track and Field

Ⓓ Running Six Miles

2. Which statement is true about track and field?

Ⓐ All runners do six-mile races.

Ⓑ It includes running, jumping, and throwing.

Ⓒ Long races are called *sprints*.

Ⓓ Track and field is a hobby.

3. How many syllables are in the word *compete*?

Ⓐ one syllable

Ⓑ two syllables

Ⓒ three syllables

Ⓓ four syllables

4. Which would probably **not** take place in a stadium?

Ⓐ a track and field meet

Ⓑ a professional baseball game

Ⓒ a school choir performance

Ⓓ a rock concert

 #50923—180 Days of Reading for Second Grade

NAME: _____ **DATE:** _____

DIRECTIONS Read the text and then answer the questions.

Most cars run on gas. Gas engines create exhaust, which makes the air dirty. This is called *pollution*. Some cars are cleaner. *Hybrids* are one example. They run on gas, but also use battery power to go. They use less gas than regular cars. This makes them better for our environment.

1. ☺ ☹

2. ☺ ☹

3. ☺ ☹

4. ☺ ☹

1. According to this text, why are hybrids better for the environment?

(A) because they run on gas

(B) because they use less gas and create less pollution

(C) because they have a gas engine

(D) because they do not make any pollution

2. What do most cars run on?

(A) electricity

(B) gas

(C) exhaust

(D) gas and electricity

3. Which word has the same root word as *pollution*?

(A) polluted

(B) poll

(C) lution

(D) ollut

4. Using context clues, what is *exhaust*?

(A) air

(B) water

(C) used gas

(D) smells

____ / 4
Total

NAME: _____ DATE: _____

The Race Track

Henry Ford is a famous man. He made cars. He formed a company. It is called the Ford Motor Company. He started it in 1903. It is still making cars today.

Cars grew more popular after Ford's company formed. More people could afford to buy them. Cars changed the way that people lived.

People have grown to love their cars. Many people drive every day. A new sport was born. Auto racing began around the 1900s. People enjoyed the thrill of a race. The National Association for Stock Car Racing (NASCAR) was formed in 1948.

The sport has changed over time. Cars have raced on dirt tracks. Now they mostly race on pavement. The shapes of the tracks have changed. They are oval. They also have steep sides. This track design helps cars go faster.

Of course, the cars go faster, too. Henry Ford might be surprised if he were alive today. His dream has taken off!

NAME:_____ DATE:_____

DIRECTIONS Read "The Race Track" and then answer the questions.

1. Which experience would help you better understand the text?

(A) I paint toy cars with my dad every weekend.

(B) I like to race bikes with my neighbor.

(C) I have watched NASCAR races on TV.

(D) When I am old enough, I will buy a motorcycle.

2. What aspect of racing tracks has changed?

(A) the snape

(B) the shape

(C) the sheep

(D) the shop

3. The shapes of the _____ have changed.

(A) tired

(B) time

(C) take

(D) tracks

4. What happened in 1948?

(A) Henry Ford died.

(B) Henry Ford started the Ford Motor Company.

(C) Henry Ford was born.

(D) NASCAR was formed.

5. Which statement gives the best summary of the text?

(A) The Ford Motor Company is still around today.

(B) NASCAR was formed in 1948.

(C) Henry Ford's invention has created a popular and thrilling sport.

(D) Henry Ford made a car that was designed for everyone.

1. ☺ ☹

2. ☺ ☹

3. ☺ ☹

4. ☺ ☹

5. ☺ ☹

____ / 5
Total

NAME:_____ **DATE:**_____

 Reread the text "The Race Track."

 Think about how there are many different kinds of races that are fun for kids to try.

Write about a time when you tried racing. What does it feel like to win or lose a race? If you have not tried racing, what kind of racing would you like to try? What do you imagine winning or losing a race would feel like?

_____

_____

_____

_____

_____

_____

_____

_____

_____

_____

_____

NAME:_____ DATE:_____

DIRECTIONS Read the text and then answer the questions.

"I want to invent a robot to have as an assistant," Nate claimed.

"What would your robot do?" his mom asked.

"It would clean my room," he said. "Actually, it would do all of my chores."

"That sounds nice! Let me know when you invent him, because I want him to do my housework, too," his mom said.

1. ☺ ☺

2. ☺ ☺

3. ☺ ☺

4. ☺ ☺

1. Who is having a conversation?

(A) Nate

(B) a mother

(C) Nate and his mother

(D) Nate and a robot

3. Which word is a compound word?

(A) wondered

(B) assistant

(C) housework

(D) actually

____ / 4
Total

2. What is the text mostly about?

(A) having an assistant

(B) doing chores

(C) plans to clean a room

(D) plans for inventing a robot

4. Which words are synonyms?

(A) *clean* and *claimed*

(B) *invent* and *assistant*

(C) *chores* and *invent*

(D) *housework* and *chores*

NAME:_____ DATE:_____

DIRECTIONS Read the text and then answer the questions.

Nina wondered if her life was easier than her parents' lives were at her age. She knew her parents' stories. She knew they did not have what she has. They had fewer channels to watch on TV. There were no video games or computers. What was life like? Nina thought about this. Is life easier with technology?

1. What does Nina wonder about?

(A) how much TV to watch

(B) whether life is easier with technology

(C) whether to buy a new computer

(D) when to watch TV

2. What is this text mostly about?

(A) a girl who complains about her hard life

(B) a girl who thinks about how technology has changed life

(C) a girl who knows her parents' stories

(D) a girl who does not like computers

3. How many syllables are in the word *technology*?

(A) five syllables

(B) two syllables

(C) three syllables

(D) four syllables

4. What would **not** be considered *technology*?

(A) video games

(B) computers

(C) cable television

(D) books

NAME:_____ **DATE:**_____

DIRECTIONS Read the text and then answer the questions.

The android was confused by what he saw as he looked through the telescope. What was this object? It had pointy ends and a handle. It looked like humans were poking their food. They used the object to stick the food into their mouths. What in the world was this crazy invention?

1. What is the invention in the text?

Ⓐ a fork
Ⓑ a knife
Ⓒ a spoon
Ⓓ chopsticks

2. How do you know the text is fantasy?

Ⓐ It is about humans.
Ⓑ It is about an android.
Ⓒ It is about a crazy invention.
Ⓓ It is about a telescope.

3. Which word has the same root word as *telescope*?

Ⓐ scoop
Ⓑ telephone
Ⓒ tell
Ⓓ tall

4. Which of the following has a *handle*?

Ⓐ a soccer ball
Ⓑ a light
Ⓒ a coffee mug
Ⓓ a chair

SCORE

1. ☺ ☺
2. ☺ ☺
3. ☺ ☺
4. ☺ ☺

____ / 4
Total

NAME:_____ DATE:_____

Into the Future

The terrain on the planet was rocky. The robots did their best to cross the field. They were trying to settle into their new home.

Problems with another robot nation had caused these robots to flee. They had the ability to fly through the air, so when the time was right, they all soared through the sky. Now they had safely landed.

The robots had their own language. It did not have words like human language. It sounded like machines working. The robots organized and created their command center. They thought they were ready for anything.

The robots did not know something. They were not alone. On the other side of the field was a large hill. On the other side of the hill was an army of creatures. Each creature had a head and six arms. Its head was covered in spikes instead of hair. It had four ears. It stood twelve feet tall. It was unlike any other creature in the universe.

The robots were not prepared. The creatures were twice as big. They were twice as strong. They were ready for war.

The robots and creatures fought. It went on day and night. At the end, the robots were badly defeated. The robots who were left flew through the air. They were going to find their next home.

NAME:_____ DATE:_____

DIRECTIONS Read "Into the Future" and then answer the questions.

1. Which shows a connection to this text?

(A) I have fights with my brothers and go to another room to get away.

(B) I was Superman for Halloween.

(C) My dad is the tallest in our family.

(D) The field at school was rocky before the grass was planted.

2. Where did the robots find other creatures?

(A) over the hull

(B) over the hall

(C) over the hill

(D) over the hole

3. What is a problem in the text?

(A) The robots fly.

(B) The robots need a new home.

(C) The robots landed safely.

(D) The planet was rocky.

4. Which best describes the robot language?

(A) There is no language.

(B) It sounds like machines working.

(C) It sounds like English.

(D) It is sign language.

5. Which best summarizes the text?

(A) The robots cannot win.

(B) The robots can fly.

(C) The robots talk.

(D) The robots are still on the move, after being defeated by creatures.

1. ☺ ☺

2. ☺ ☺

3. ☺ ☺

4. ☺ ☺

5. ☺ ☺

____ / 5
Total

NAME: _____ **DATE:** _____

 Reread the text "Into the Future."

 Think about how the robots seem to have a hard time finding a place to be comfortable.

Write about a time when you have been uncomfortable somewhere. What did you do about it?

_____

_____

_____

_____

_____

_____

_____

_____

_____

_____

_____

_____

_____

NAME:_____ DATE:_____

DIRECTIONS Read the text and then answer the questions.

A person who is blind cannot see. People can lose their vision for a lot of reasons. Some people are born blind, and others lose their sight after an accident or illness. People who are blind must learn how to get around in the world. They can read using *braille*. This is a system of raised dots that are read by touch.

1. ☺ ☺

2. ☺ ☺

3. ☺ ☺

4. ☺ ☺

1. What is this text mostly about?

Ⓐ accidents

Ⓑ raised dots

Ⓒ being blind

Ⓓ reading braille

3. Which word is a compound word?

Ⓐ raised

Ⓑ system

Ⓒ illness

Ⓓ become

____ / 4
Total

2. How do people become blind?

Ⓐ People become blind after an accident.

Ⓑ People are born blind.

Ⓒ People become blind after an illness.

Ⓓ all of the above

4. Which words are synonyms?

Ⓐ *vision* and *sight*

Ⓑ *touch* and *read*

Ⓒ *blind* and *braille*

Ⓓ *world* and *around*

NAME:_____ DATE:_____

SCORE

1. ☺ ☹

2. ☺ ☹

3. ☺ ☹

4. ☺ ☹

___/ 4
Total

DIRECTIONS Read the text and then answer the questions.

Sign language is a way to share ideas. It is used by and for people who are deaf. Deaf people cannot hear. Sign language is a way to express ideas with hands. Gestures are used instead of spoken words.

1. What is a fact about sign language?

(A) It does not work as well as spoken language.

(B) It is a way to share ideas.

(C) It is only for deaf people.

(D) It is only for blind people.

2. What fact about sign language is **not** included in the text?

(A) It uses gestures instead of spoken words.

(B) It is used for and by people who are deaf.

(C) It helps strengthen hand muscles.

(D.) It is a way to express ideas with hands.

3. Which has the same vowel sound as *deaf*?

(A) deep

(B) fed

(C) bead

(D) leaf

4. What is an example of a *gesture*?

(A) watching television

(B) yelling, "I love you!"

(C) a wave to say goodbye

(D) reading a book

#50923—180 Days of Reading for Second Grade   © Shell Education

NAME:_____ DATE:_____

DIRECTIONS Read the text and then answer the questions.

Some books are about real people. They are *biographies*. They tell a life story. A life story can teach a lesson. It may inspire others. We can learn from each other. Readers like good stories about real people.

1. ☺ ☺

2. ☺ ☺

1. What is the main idea?

(A) Life stories are inspiring.

(B) A biography is a person's life story that others can learn from.

(C) Good stories teach lessons.

(D) A life story might not be similar to your own life.

2. Readers enjoy biographies because

(A) they are about people who are alive.

(B) they are short.

(C) they like stories about real people.

(D) they are easy to read.

3. Which word has the same prefix as *biography*?

(A) biology

(B) telegraph

(C) autograph

(D) grape

4. Which word is a synonym for *inspire*?

(A) sadden

(B) motivate

(C) anger

(D) upset

3. ☺ ☺

4. ☺ ☺

_____ / 4
Total

NAME:_____ DATE:_____

The Life of Helen Keller

Helen Keller was born in 1880. She was a healthy baby. The first year of her life was normal. One day, she had a very high fever. She got really sick. She lost her sight. She also lost her hearing. She was blind and deaf.

Helen grew very frustrated. She could not hear. She could not see. She could not talk to people. Helen began to have horrible tantrums.

Helen's family needed help. They hired a teacher. Anne Sullivan became Helen's teacher. She taught Helen many things. She taught her new words. She helped Helen connect ideas. This helped Helen learn to speak. She was six years old. She felt Anne's lips as she talked. Helen copied Anne. Anne was not always easy to understand. Yet Helen never gave up.

Helen worked hard her entire life. She grew to be an amazing woman. She went to college. She wrote books. She traveled the world. She did not let anything stop her.

Perhaps Helen's greatest gift was teaching others to respect her. She wanted respect for all people who are blind or deaf. She shared her life with others. Helen Keller died in 1968. She lived a full life. She was a hero to many people.

Helen Keller

NAME:_____ **DATE:**_____

DIRECTIONS   Read "The Life of Helen Keller" and then answer the questions.

1. Who might make a connection to the text?

(A) an author who has written many books

(B) a mother who has a sick baby

(C) a child who wears leg braces but wants to learn to play soccer

(D) a student who learns from a teacher

2. What did Anne Sullivan teach Helen?

(A) worries

(B) words

(C) wards

(D) worms

3. What word best describes Helen Keller?

(A) healthy

(B) shy

(C) hero

(D) horrible

4. Which best describes how Helen Keller lived her life?

(A) She worked with Anne Sullivan.

(B) She spoke new words.

(C) She lived a full life even though she was deaf and blind.

(D) She traveled the world.

5. Which gives the best summary of the text?

(A) Helen Keller learned many new things, including how to talk and how to read braille.

(B) Helen Keller was deaf and blind.

(C) Helen Keller worked hard her entire life.

(D) Helen Keller overcame being deaf and blind to have a good life and earn the respect of others.

1. ☺ ☺

2. ☺ ☺

3. ☺ ☺

4. ☺ ☺

5. ☺ ☺

___ / 5
Total

NAME:_____ DATE:_____

SCORE

___/4

 Reread the text "The Life of Helen Keller."

 Think about the courage of Helen Keller. She had to overcome a lot.

 Write about what has helped build your courage. When have you had to overcome something and be brave?

_____

_____

_____

_____

_____

_____

_____

_____

_____

_____

NAME:_____ DATE:_____

DIRECTIONS Read the text and then answer the questions.

> I wanted some items at my party. Balloons are fun. They are a nice decoration. Streamers look pretty, too. I picked a purple birthday cake. Cupcakes would have been okay, too. My mom is getting the candles. They tell everyone how old I am turning!

1. ☺ ☹

2. ☺ ☹

1. Who is the narrator?

Ⓐ a child celebrating a birthday

Ⓑ a dad making dinner

Ⓒ a party guest

Ⓓ a mother

3. Which word is a compound word?

Ⓐ candle

Ⓑ balloon

Ⓒ turning

Ⓓ cupcake

3. ☺ ☹

4. ☺ ☹

___ / 4

Total

2. What does the text tell the reader about this birthday party?

Ⓐ Only moms can get the candles.

Ⓑ It includes decorations and yummy treats.

Ⓒ Cupcakes are better than a cake.

Ⓓ Parties last a long time.

4. What does the narrator mean by saying that candles *tell everyone how old I am turning*?

Ⓐ The number of candles on the cake matches the age of the narrator.

Ⓑ Candles have signs on them telling a person's age.

Ⓒ Moms announce your age at the party.

Ⓓ Trick candles won't blow out.

NAME: _____ **DATE:** _____

DIRECTIONS Read the text and then answer the questions.

Hank had to pick his team for a game of kickball. Hank was one captain, and Felix was the other captain. They took their time choosing the players they each wanted. It was hard to exclude people, but Hank and Felix both wanted to win. They did not want to pick the kids who could not play.

1. Who are the kickball captains?

- (A) Hank and Chloe
- (B) Felix and Juan
- (C) Hank and Felix
- (D) There were no captains.

2. What is the text mostly about?

- (A) winning
- (B) captains picking teams for kickball
- (C) excluding kids
- (D) Hank

3. Which two words could make a compound word?

- (A) *win* and *game*
- (B) *pick* and *team*
- (C) *play* and *game*
- (D) *play* and *time*

4. What is an example of how kids can *exclude* others?

- (A) only eating lunch with certain kids and sending others away
- (B) working on a class group project
- (C) reading a book together in the library
- (D) playing chase at recess

NAME:_____ **DATE:**_____

DIRECTIONS Read the text and then answer the questions.

Kayla felt alone. Her two friends were on the bars at recess. Other kids in her class were chasing one another. She was not interested in the games. Kayla decided to sit by herself and watch. Some days she felt sad on the playground. She worried about finding her friends. She never knew what to play.

1. ☺ 😐

2. ☺ 😐

3. ☺ 😐

4. ☺ 😐

____ / 4
Total

1. What is the setting?

(A) the playground

(B) the classroom

(C) the school gym

(D) the street

2. Which title best fits the text?

(A) Swinging on the Bars

(B) Sunny Play Day

(C) No Chase Game Today

(D) A Rough Time at Recess

3. Which word is a compound word?

(A) finding

(B) chasing

(C) worried

(D) herself

4. Which would kids **not** be doing on the bars at recess?

(A) swinging

(B) kicking

(C) twirling

(D) hanging

NAME:_____ DATE:_____

Making the Guest List

George could not wait for his birthday party. He had been planning it for months, and he knew exactly what he wanted to do. He wanted to go to the batting cages with his friends. Baseball was George's favorite sport, and he knew his friends would love to practice with him.

A few weeks before the party, George got his guest list in order. He had seven friends that he wanted to invite. He wrote up the invitations. He brought them to school to pass out. His plan was working out nicely.

The day before the party, his mom got a phone call. It was the owner of the batting cages. They were just checking on the plan. But there was a problem. They only had room for five kids. Not all of the kids would be able to practice. George could not believe it. He had no idea how to choose. Who would play? Who would sit out?

George talked to his mom. He knew what he had to do. George changed the plans. It was more important to him to include everyone. He could go to the batting cages another time. Instead, the children headed to the movies. All of them went as a group. Everyone had a great time—especially George!

#50923—180 Days of Reading for Second Grade

NAME: _____ **DATE:** _____

DIRECTIONS Read "Making the Guest List" and then answer the questions.

1. Who might make a connection to the text?

(A) an owner of batting cages

(B) a person who sells birthday invitations

(C) a child who hates baseball

(D) a child who invites a whole class to her party

2. What did George get in order?

(A) a list

(B) a lost

(C) a last

(D) a fist

3. What are batting cages?

(A) They are places for large birthday parties.

(B) They are animal homes.

(C) They are places to practice batting.

(D) They are not fun.

4. What is the problem?

(A) George loved movies.

(B) George could not play baseball well.

(C) George invited too many birthday guests to do his favorite activity.

(D) George invited the wrong kids to his party.

5. Which word best summarizes George's actions?

(A) confusing

(B) considerate

(C) selfish

(D) rude

1. ☺ ☹

2. ☺ ☹

3. ☺ ☹

4. ☺ ☹

5. ☺ ☹

___ / 5

Total

NAME: _____ DATE: _____

SCORE
___ / 4

Reread the text "Making the Guest List."

Think about the decision that George made.

Write about a time when you did something to make sure people's feelings were not hurt.

_____

_____

_____

_____

_____

_____

_____

_____

_____

_____

_____

NAME: _____   DATE: _____

DIRECTIONS Read the text and then answer the questions.

> A new video game was shown in 1958. It was called *Tennis for Two*. It was a first. People had never seen a game like this. It was played on a screen. This was amazing. It was a new invention. It led to many new video games. People are still playing video games today.

1. ☺ ☹

2. ☺ ☹

1. What is the most important idea?

Ⓐ *Tennis for Two* was shown in 1958.

Ⓑ *Tennis for Two* was amazing.

Ⓒ *Tennis for Two* was the first of many video games.

Ⓓ *Tennis for Two* was about tennis.

2. What did *Tennis for Two* lead to?

Ⓐ a real tennis game

Ⓑ a new game on a screen

Ⓒ more video games

Ⓓ *Tennis for Three*

3. Which word has a suffix, or word ending?

Ⓐ video

Ⓑ playing

Ⓒ people

Ⓓ today

3. ☺ ☹

4. ☺ ☹

4. Which definition of *led* is used in the text?

Ⓐ moved in a direction

Ⓑ directed

Ⓒ was the leader

Ⓓ guided

___ / 4

Total

NAME: _____ **DATE:** _____

DIRECTIONS Read the text and then answer the questions.

1. ☺ ☺

2. ☺ ☺

Children used to play outside a lot. It was what they did for fun. Today, children watch a lot of television. No one agrees on how much television is healthy for a child. Children look at computers and play video games as well. This all adds up to more screen time than ever.

3. ☺ ☺

1. **Which title best fits the text?**

 (A) Screen Time

 (B) Playing Outside

 (C) An Unhealthy Habit

 (D) What Is Fun?

4. ☺ ☺

___ / 4
Total

2. **What is the big change described in the text?**

 (A) Kids never play outside.

 (B) Kids are in front of screens more than ever.

 (C) Screen time is making kids sad.

 (D) Screens are getting larger.

3. **What is the suffix, or word ending, in the word *computers*?**

 (A) *com–*

 (B) *–rs*

 (C) *–puters*

 (D) *–ers*

4. **What does the phrase *screen time* mean in the text?**

 (A) time spent in front of a screen

 (B) a clock on the screen

 (C) the type of screen

 (D) the size of a screen

NAME:_____   DATE:_____

DIRECTIONS   Read the text and then answer the questions.

Internet users must be smart. Children have to know how to move around a website. They must be able to search online. They also must watch what they post online. Children should never chat with strangers online. Having a parent nearby to help is a good idea.

1. 🙂 ☹

2. 🙂 😐

1. Which idea is **not** included in the text?

Ⓐ An adult should help kids use the Internet.

Ⓑ Strangers are on the Internet.

Ⓒ Kids need to know how to be smart on the Internet.

Ⓓ Getting around online is very easy.

2. What is **not** something that kids must know about going online?

Ⓐ how to move around a website

Ⓑ how to watch what they post

Ⓒ how to chat with strangers

Ⓓ how to search online

3. Which word has the same suffix as the word *having*?

Ⓐ shaved

Ⓑ have

Ⓒ taking

Ⓓ cave

4. Which of these words mean the same thing?

Ⓐ *nearby* and *smart*

Ⓑ *online* and *Internet*

Ⓒ *parent* and *kids*

Ⓓ *move* and *search*

3. 🙂 ☹

4. 🙂 😐

____ / 4
Total

NAME:_____ DATE:_____

A New Kind of Game

Older people grew up playing different games than what children play today. Board games were a lot of fun. Monopoly was popular many years ago. So were checkers and chess. Marbles have been around for a long time. Children today still play those games. Yet they also play a new kind of game.

Video games have grown more popular over the past few decades. Arcade games were a big hit in the 1970s and 1980s. This also was the birth of computer games. More children had access to these new screens. They were hooked. The games were fast and fun. A lot of action happened on the screen at one time. Plus, many of the games could be played solo. A player could go up against the computer. That was a fun challenge.

Children loved playing video games. Many did not have video games in their own homes. They had to go to an arcade. Sometimes, friends would gather at a house. They would all share the video games there.

Over time, it was more common for people to have their own games at home. Video-game screens also shrank. They went from a large screen in an arcade to a small screen in your hand.

It is hard to know what will be next. What will be the great game of the future?

NAME:_____ DATE:_____

DIRECTIONS Read "A New Kind of Game" and then answer the questions.

1. Which shows a connection to the text?

(A) I want to read books in my free time.

(B) Looking at small screens hurts my eyes.

(C) I enjoy playing many kinds of games, including video games.

(D) I don't know the rules of Monopoly.

2. How does the author describe arcade games when they were first invented?

(A) a big hut

(B) a big hat

(C) a bit hot

(D) a big hit

3. Which definition of *birth* is used?

(A) related by blood

(B) a new baby being born

(C) a person's heritage

(D) the start of something

4. What is explained in this text?

(A) the rules of Monopoly

(B) the shrinking size of video games

(C) the history of games

(D) games of the future

5. Which best summarizes the text?

(A) Arcade games are very large.

(B) Video games are for boys.

(C) Video games have grown more popular.

(D) Video games bring children together.

1. ☺ ☹

2. ☺ ☹

3. ☺ ☹

4. ☺ ☹

5. ☺ ☹

___ / 5
Total

NAME: _____ DATE: _____

📘 **Reread** the text "A New Kind of Game."

 Think about how the games that children like to play are changing all the time.

 Write about the kind of game you would invent for the future.

_____

_____

_____

_____

_____

_____

_____

_____

_____

_____

NAME:_____ **DATE:**_____

DIRECTIONS Read the text and then answer the questions.

Luis needed a new suit. His aunt was getting married the next day. Luis and his mother went to the mall. They were shopping for new clothes. Luis was miserable. He was distracted. All he could think about was playing ball with his friends. He hated being inside on such a beautiful day.

1. ☺ ☹

2. ☺ ☹

3. ☺ ☹

4. ☺ ☹

____ / 4
Total

1. When does the text take place?

(A) on Luis's birthday

(B) on a snowy day

(C) on the day before a wedding

(D) on the day of Luis's baseball practice

2. What is the main idea?

(A) Luis has to shop when he would rather be outside playing ball.

(B) Luis has an aunt who is getting married.

(C) Luis likes to play ball.

(D) It is a beautiful day.

3. What is the compound word in the text?

(A) inside

(B) married

(C) mother

(D) needed

4. What is the meaning of the word *miserable*?

(A) lonely

(B) very unhappy

(C) skinny

(D) confused

NAME: _____ DATE: _____

SCORE

DIRECTIONS Read the text and then answer the questions.

1. ☺ ☹

2. ☺ ☹

> Brady really wanted to learn how to ride his bike. All of his friends were able to ride bikes, and he felt excluded. Brady had been trying all summer. He was not having much luck. His dad suggested they go to the park. He thought the wide, open space would be helpful. He was right, and Brady rode right away!

3. ☺ ☹

4. ☺ ☹

_____ / 4
Total

1. What solution does Brady's dad suggest?

Ⓐ to practice on his bike more

Ⓑ to go to the park and practice in the wide, open space

Ⓒ to join his friends

Ⓓ to take a break

2. Which title best fits the text?

Ⓐ Keeping Up with Friends

Ⓑ Don't Give Up

Ⓒ Summer Fun

Ⓓ Bad Luck

3. What other word has the same suffix as *helpful*?

Ⓐ helping

Ⓑ wishful

Ⓒ full

Ⓓ helper

4. What is an example of a person being *excluded*?

Ⓐ a family having dinner together

Ⓑ a classmate not being picked for a game

Ⓒ two puppies playing together

Ⓓ a friend giving out party invitations

NAME: _____ **DATE:** _____

DIRECTIONS Read the text and then answer the questions.

Hannah read the newspaper. She was curious. Hannah learned about her town. She read about events on her street. She found out about a new stop sign. It was being placed on the corner. The newspaper taught Hannah about her community.

1. ☺ ☺

2. ☺ ☺

1. What does Hannah read about in a newspaper?

(A) her town

(B) a school

(C) a corner

(D) a letter

2. What is the most important idea about newspapers?

(A) They write about stop signs.

(B) They are good for children to read.

(C) They tell people more about their community.

(D) They are interesting for curious people.

3. Which word has the same root word as *placed*?

(A) play

(B) replace

(C) lace

(D) lacy

4. Which is **not** found in a newspaper?

(A) stories

(B) photographs

(C) advertisements

(D) menus

3. ☺ ☺

4. ☺ ☺

____ / 4
Total

NAME: _____ DATE: _____

Save Our Park!

November 2, 2012

Dear Editor,

 I have lived in Jackson my entire life. I go to Lake School. I am in second grade. I am writing this letter because I do not agree with your article. You wrote about the new shopping mall that will be built on First Street. I think it is exciting to have new things to do here. I just wish our city did not decide to get rid of Hardy Park. Why should we lose a park to get a mall?

 Parks are important to everyone who lives here. Kids like to play in them. Adults can relax with their families. They are great places to walk dogs and get exercise. Grown-ups are always telling kids to get more exercise. Are we supposed to get our exercise at the mall now?

 Shopping is fun. Exercise is important. I think it is a big mistake to get rid of our park. Some people say that our town has many other parks. This is true. But each park is important. Let us keep the park and find another spot for the mall.

Sincerely,

Jamie Smith

NAME:_____ **DATE:**_____

DIRECTIONS Read "Save Our Park!" and then answer the questions.

1. Who might make a connection to the text?

(A) a student who does not like the principal at Lake School

(B) a radio announcer in Jackson

(C) people who appreciate nature in their town or city

(D) a girl who enjoys shopping at the mall

2. Jamie doesn't want the city to get ____ of a park.

(A) rid

(B) rig

(C) rod

(D) rad

3. What is one reason to keep Hardy Park?

(A) Shopping is fun.

(B) Parks are pretty.

(C) People exercise at the park.

(D) There are other parks.

4. Jamie's letter

(A) impresses her teacher.

(B) shares her opinions about parks.

(C) stops the mall from being built.

(D) gives her exercise.

5. What is Jamie's main point in her letter?

(A) Jamie has lived in Jackson her entire life.

(B) Hardy Park is old.

(C) A park is more important to the town than a mall.

(D) A mall keeps people from exercising.

1. ☺ ☺

2. ☺ ☺

3. ☺ ☺

4. ☺ ☺

5. ☺ ☺

___ / 5
Total

NAME: _____ **DATE:** _____

 **Reread** the text "Save Our Park!"

 Think about how Jamie decided to do something about her problem and how she wrote a letter to the newspaper to share her opinion.

 Write about a problem you would like solved in your community. How would you describe the issue in a letter to the newspaper?

_____

_____

_____

_____

_____

_____

_____

_____

_____

_____

NAME: _____ **DATE:** _____

DIRECTIONS Read the text and then answer the questions.

> Have you ever heard of the Eiffel Tower? It is a famous building. It is in Paris, France. It is a beautiful monument. It was built in 1889. It took more than two years to build it! Many visitors go to the tower each year. It lights up at night. What a sight!

1. ☺ ☹

2. ☺ ☹

3. ☺ ☹

4. ☺ ☹

1. Which sentence best sums up the text?

(A) The Eiffel Tower gets many visitors.

(B) The Eiffel Tower lights up at night.

(C) The Eiffel Tower is a famous building in Paris that many people visit.

(D) The Eiffel Tower took two years to build.

2. Which statement is **not** true about the Eiffel Tower?

(A) It took less than two years to build.

(B) It is a famous building.

(C) It is in Paris, France.

(D) It was built in 1889.

3. Which words have the same vowel sound?

(A) *two* and *tower*

(B) *lights* and *sight*

(C) *took* and *more*

(D) *heard* and *each*

4. What is another term for *monument*?

(A) light

(B) famous building

(C) French

(D) street

____ / 4
Total

NAME: _____ **DATE:** _____

DIRECTIONS Read the text and then answer the questions.

Most people buy things with money. They use bills and coins. They shop for what they need. This is true in places around the world. Most countries have their own type of money. A *dollar* is a bill in America. A *euro* is money spent in parts of Europe. People who travel have to exchange money. They have to use the money of the country they are visiting.

1. What is the text mostly about?

(A) exchanging money

(B) money

(C) euros

(D) shopping

2. Which type of money is compared to a *dollar*?

(A) a euro

(B) a bill

(C) a coin

(D) money

3. Which words have the same vowel sound?

(A) *buy* and *true*

(B) *use* and *around*

(C) *country* and *money*

(D) *spent* and *people*

4. Which is **not** a word in the text that has to do with *money*?

(A) spent

(B) shop

(C) buy

(D) places

NAME: _____ **DATE:** _____

DIRECTIONS Read the text and then answer the questions.

What is a *continent*? It is a large area of land. There are seven continents in the world. A continent may be divided into many countries. It may have dozens. One continent has only one country. Which one is it? It is Australia.

1. ☺ ☺

2. ☺ ☺

1. What is **not** true about continents?

(A) Australia is a continent.

(B) The world is divided into these large areas of land.

(C) They are divided into smaller countries.

(D) There are eight of them.

3. Which has the same root word as *divided*?

(A) video

(B) division

(C) vice

(D) dive

3. ☺ ☺

4. ☺ ☺

___ / 4
Total

2. What is unique about Australia?

(A) It is a continent.

(B) It is a country.

(C) It is both a continent and a country.

(D) It is neither a continent nor a country.

4. How might you learn more about *continents*?

(A) by looking up at the sky

(B) by reading a math book

(C) by listening to music

(D) by looking at a map

NAME:_____   DATE:_____

France

France is a country. It is in Europe. The capital of France is Paris. It is a beautiful part of the world. France is one of the oldest nations. Evidence shows humans settled there over 16,000 years ago!

The landscape is very diverse. There are warm beaches in the south. They are found on the Mediterranean Sea. The French Riviera is there. It is famous for its beaches. There are also huge mountains. They are the French Alps. France has a lot of land for growing crops, too. The country makes many food items. A lot of these are shipped around the world. France is famous for wine and cheese products.

Many people want to visit France. About 75 million people visit every year. They love the beaches. They visit the mountains. They also flock to Paris. This famous city has a lot to offer. French food is delicious. People like to walk around the beautiful city. They enjoy the sights. They shop and eat.

Paris, France

You might visit France one day. If you do, try to learn a few words in French. Then you can talk to people there.

NAME: _____ **DATE:** _____

DIRECTIONS Read "France" and then answer the questions.

1. Which statement shows a connection to the text?

(A) Cheese makes my stomach hurt.

(B) My family goes on trips and we learn as much as we can about places.

(C) I like the beach.

(D) I can say a few words in Spanish.

2. What does France grow and ship?

(A) crocs

(B) crops

(C) chops

(D) clops

3. What does *flock* mean in the third paragraph?

(A) a group of birds

(B) visit in large numbers

(C) fake snow

(D) leave

4. Which part of French life is **not** in the text?

(A) its tourism business

(B) its landscape

(C) its history

(D) its government

5. Which gives the best summary of the text?

(A) France is a beautiful country with a lot of interesting things to see and do.

(B) You must choose whether to visit the mountains or the beach in France.

(C) France is a very old country.

(D) Speaking French will make your visit easier.

1. ☺ ☺
2. ☺ ☺
3. ☺ ☺
4. ☺ ☺
5. ☺ ☺

___ / 5
Total

NAME: _____ **DATE:** _____

 Reread the text "France."

 Think about all that you have learned about France.

✏️ **Write about** the feature of France that is most interesting to you, and why.

_____

_____

_____

_____

_____

_____

_____

_____

_____

_____

_____

_____

NAME: _____ **DATE:** _____

DIRECTIONS Read the text and then answer the questions.

The time machine was turned on, and now Ella had a choice. Which year did she want to visit? She could go to the past or she could go to the future. She could try to meet someone famous. At first, Ella had a hard time deciding. She finally knew what to do. She wanted to see ancient Rome for herself.

1. ☺ 😐

2. ☺ 😐

3. ☺ 😐

4. ☺ 😐

1. What is the text mostly about?

- Ⓐ a vacation
- Ⓑ an airplane ride
- Ⓒ a time machine
- Ⓓ Rome

2. How do you know the text is fiction?

- Ⓐ because ancient Rome is about history
- Ⓑ because a time machine is make-believe
- Ⓒ because Ella is by herself
- Ⓓ because it is about the future

3. Which is a compound word?

- Ⓐ someone
- Ⓑ finally
- Ⓒ wanted
- Ⓓ machine

4. If Ella traveled to *ancient* Rome, which would be true?

- Ⓐ Ella traveled to an island.
- Ⓑ Ella traveled to a castle.
- Ⓒ Ella traveled to the future.
- Ⓓ Ella traveled to the past.

____ / 4

Total

NAME:_____ DATE:_____

SCORE

1. ☺ ☻

2. ☺ ☻

3. ☺ ☻

4. ☺ ☻

____/ 4
Total

DIRECTIONS Read the text and then answer the questions.

"What do you think this is?" the little girl asked her friend. The two girls were at the park and had wandered off beyond the playground. They were in new territory. They noticed a large, purple mushroom.

"I don't know what that is," said the friend. The two girls touched it, and in an instant, they disappeared into thin air.

1. What happens after the girls touch the mushroom?

(A) They leave the park.

(B) They disappear.

(C) They go to a new territory.

(D) They leave the playground.

2. Which title best fits the text?

(A) The Wandering Girls

(B) A Day at the Park

(C) The Journey

(D) A Magical Moment

3. Which word has the same prefix as *disappeared*?

(A) disapprove

(B) appreciate

(C) appearance

(D) apparently

4. Where should young children **not** be allowed to *wander*?

(A) a garden

(B) a school playground

(C) a busy city street

(D) a backyard

NAME:_____ **DATE:**_____

DIRECTIONS Read the text and then answer the questions.

The map had a large X on it. The woman who found it had turned it in to the hotel front desk. She said that the map was rolled up and lying on the sandy beach. The hotel owner took the map and set it aside. He did not think any more about the map. The owner's son was much more curious. He knew it was a map to a buried treasure.

1. ☺ ☹

2. ☺ ☹

3. ☺ ☹

4. ☺ ☹

____ / 4
Total

1. What does the owner's son think he has found?

Ⓐ a buried treasure

Ⓑ a map to a buried treasure

Ⓒ a map with an X on it

Ⓓ a map to the hotel

2. What is the most important part of the text?

Ⓐ A hotel owner put a map aside.

Ⓑ A boy saw a map and thought it might lead him to a buried treasure.

Ⓒ A map had an X on it.

Ⓓ A map was rolled up.

3. Which two words have the same suffix?

Ⓐ *sandy* and *front*

Ⓑ *aside* and *map*

Ⓒ *turned* and *buried*

Ⓓ *rolled* and *hotel*

4. What does the phrase *turned it in* mean in the text?

Ⓐ handed over a lost item

Ⓑ repaid something

Ⓒ said something again

Ⓓ turned something inside out

NAME:_____ DATE:_____

The Mystery Box

Zoe and Liam were playing in the backyard. It was a very typical day for the two siblings. Zoe was playing in the sandbox, and Liam was practicing baseball. The sun was about to set, so their mom was going to call them in for dinner at any moment.

Liam stopped quickly. He noticed something in the corner of the yard. He had never seen it before. It was stuck between two trees and a bush. It was the corner of a large box. The box was turned on its side. It was buried. The corner of the box was sticking out slightly.

Liam told Zoe about it, so they went to check it out. Zoe was worried it was something scary, but Liam was excited. He thought it was an interesting discovery.

The two of them opened the box. Inside was a pile of old cloth. The kids were so confused. Liam was hoping for a treasure. Zoe was worried about seeing something gross. But a pile of cloth? Why was that in this box?

They pulled the long strips of white cloth out. They started to lay it out on the ground. Zoe thought she smelled something odd. Liam kept working.

After a few minutes the kids looked closely at the cloth. A few pieces of cloth had imprints on them. It looked like a face. Zoe could see the outline of a nose and eyes.

Liam wondered if the cloth was wrapped around a person. Zoe thought about this. She sat up quickly. A look of terror was in her eyes. Did they just find the cloth of a mummy?

NAME:_____ DATE:_____

DIRECTIONS Read "The Mystery Box" and then answer the questions.

1. Who might make a connection to the text?

(A) a child who has discovered things in his own backyard

(B) a child who enjoys reading about trees

(C) a person who designs boxes

(D) a gardener

2. What is buried?

(A) a toy

(B) a box

(C) a bag

(D) a treasure

3. What does a *typical day* mean for Zoe and Liam?

(A) a day spent arguing

(B) a day doing things they usually do

(C) a day spent typing

(D) a day spent inside

4. What is Zoe and Liam's relationship?

(A) They are neighbors.

(B) They are brother and sister.

(C) They are friends.

(D) They are strangers.

5. Which gives the best summary of the text?

(A) Two kids discover a box and are too afraid to open it.

(B) Two kids discover a box and argue about what to do.

(C) Two kids play in the backyard.

(D) Two kids discover a box that is full of cloth, and think it may have come from a mummy.

1. ☺ ☺

2. ☺ ☺

3. ☺ ☺

4. ☺ ☺

5. ☺ ☺

___ / 5

Total

NAME:_____ DATE:_____

 Reread the text "The Mystery Box."

 Think about finding a mystery box in your own backyard.

 Write about what you would do with it.

_____

_____

_____

_____

_____

_____

_____

_____

_____

_____

_____

NAME:_____ **DATE:**_____

DIRECTIONS Read the text and then answer the questions.

> A roller coaster can be a real thrill! It is a very fun ride. Did you know that science teaches us how a roller coaster works? A roller coaster is not run by an engine. It is pulled to the top of a hill, and then it is let go. The *momentum* (moh-MEN-tuhm) from rolling down the hill keeps the roller coaster moving.

1. ☺ ☺

2. ☺ ☺

3. ☺ ☺

4. ☺ ☺

____ / 4
Total

1. What is the text mostly about?

Ⓐ science

Ⓑ amusement parks

Ⓒ roller coasters

Ⓓ hills

2. How does a roller coaster keep moving?

Ⓐ momentum

Ⓑ an engine

Ⓒ electricity

Ⓓ horsepower

3. How many syllables are in the word *momentum*?

Ⓐ five syllables

Ⓑ two syllables

Ⓒ three syllables

Ⓓ four syllables

4. Using context clues, which definition of *momentum* makes the most sense?

Ⓐ gravity

Ⓑ having speed

Ⓒ reverse speed

Ⓓ length

NAME:_____ DATE:_____

DIRECTIONS Read the text and then answer the questions.

A *balance* is a simple device. It is for weighing objects. It was the first type of scale invented. An object of unknown weight is placed on one side. Then, a known amount of weight is put on the other side. The balance will be equal when both sides have the same amount of weight.

1. What is a good title for the text?

(A) A Balancing Beam

(B) Heavy Things

(C) All About Scales

(D) The First Scale

2. When does the balance become equal?

(A) when you first put weight on one side

(B) when both sides have an equal amount of weight

(C) when both sides have different weight

(D) when your known weight is more

3. What is the root word in *unknown*?

(A) own

(B) know

(C) now

(D) unknow

4. What word in the text is similar to *balance*?

(A) equation

(B) difference

(C) scale

(D) object

NAME: _____ **DATE:** _____

DIRECTIONS Read the text and then answer the questions.

A top is a toy that has been around for a long time. It is spun while it balances on a point. Usually, a player's fingers grab the top and give it a twirl. Sometimes, a string or stick is used to make the toy spin. When the top slows down, it topples onto a surface.

1. ☺ ☺

2. ☺ ☺

3. ☺ ☺

4. ☺ ☺

___ / 4
Total

1. What is the most important idea?

(A) A top is a toy that spins while balancing on a point.

(B) The top has been around for a long time.

(C) A top is twirled with fingers.

(D) A top always topples down.

2. What is **not** used to spin a top?

(A) a string

(B) a stick

(C) a battery

(D) fingers

3. Which two words make a compound word?

(A) *down* and *long*

(B) *toy* and *time*

(C) *point* and *string*

(D) *down* and *time*

4. Which two words are similar in meaning?

(A) *balances* and *make*

(B) *spin* and *twirl*

(C) *slows* and *grab*

(D) *point* and *surface*

NAME: _____ DATE: _____

Constant Motion

Things are moving around us all of the time. Cars and bikes zoom by. Balls roll away. Waves come and go. Even our own planet is revolving and rotating. It does this and we don't even feel it!

Many things move in some way. Yet objects do not all move in the same way. Motion can mean a lot of things. It can mean moving from one place to another. It can mean spinning around in the same spot. Some objects balance and then begin to move. They may topple over in the end.

People are fascinated by motion. Even babies like to watch things move. Many parents hang a mobile over their baby's crib. Babies find the movement interesting.

As kids grow up, they love to move things around. Toy cars can zoom fast on a track. Towers of blocks can be balanced carefully. Then the blocks fall over and collapse. Paper airplanes are fun to fly through the air.

Adults study motion, too. They learn how to keep airplanes moving through the sky. They follow rules for moving safely on streets and freeways. They design toys and machines. All of these move, too.

Look around you right now. What do you see that is moving?

NAME:_____ DATE:_____

DIRECTIONS Read "Constant Motion" and then answer the questions.

1. Which shows a connection to the text?

(A) Cars drive too fast on the freeway.

(B) I want to learn how to ride a bike.

(C) I don't remember sleeping in a crib.

(D) I practice balancing and turning in ballet class.

2. How do balls move?

(A) They rail.

(B) They rule.

(C) They roar.

(D) They roll.

3. Which shows the author's opinion?

(A) All things move the same way.

(B) Children like motion.

(C) Adults do not care for motion.

(D) Balance is important.

4. Which verb is **not** used in the text?

(A) crawl

(B) zoom

(C) roll

(D) fly

5. Which gives the best summary of the text?

(A) Objects move in a straight line.

(B) Objects don't always move.

(C) Objects move in many ways.

(D) Objects move fast or slowly.

1. ☺ ☹

2. ☺ ☹

3. ☺ ☹

4. ☺ ☹

5. ☺ ☹

___ / 5
Total

NAME:_____ DATE:_____

 Reread the text "Constant Motion."

 Think about an experience that you have had with motion.

Write about what was moving. How would you describe the motion? Why do you remember this?

_____

_____

_____

_____

_____

_____

_____

_____

_____

_____

_____

_____

NAME: _____ **DATE:** _____

DIRECTIONS Read the text and then answer the questions.

Justin saw the large, hairy spider. It crawled out from behind the cupboard. He screamed and ran out of the kitchen. "What is wrong?" his mother shouted. Justin was afraid to tell his mom. She had a phobia of spiders. She would not be happy to see the one thing she feared the most.

1. ☺ ☺

2. ☺ ☺

3. ☺ ☺

4. ☺ ☺

1. What happens right after Justin sees the spider?

Ⓐ Justin looks in the cupboard.

Ⓑ Justin screams and runs out of the kitchen.

Ⓒ Justin tells his mom about the spider.

Ⓓ Justin's mom shouts.

2. What is the main idea?

Ⓐ A spider is large and hairy.

Ⓑ Justin's mom has a phobia.

Ⓒ Justin spots a spider and doesn't want to tell his mom.

Ⓓ Justin screams.

3. What is the compound word in the text?

Ⓐ afraid

Ⓑ cupboard

Ⓒ hairy

Ⓓ kitchen

4. What is the meaning of the word *phobia*?

Ⓐ a scream

Ⓑ related to spiders

Ⓒ a strong fear

Ⓓ something that makes you unhappy

___ / 4
Total

NAME: _____ **DATE:**_____

DIRECTIONS Read the text and then answer the questions.

A lot of things happen during my school day. My teacher keeps us busy. We read and write every morning. I like writing in journals and reading independently. Morning recess is a good break from our work. Then it is time for math. We work hard until it is time for lunch. In the afternoon, we may do science, social studies, or art. The bell rings at three o'clock. We sure pack a lot into one school day!

1. Who is the narrator?

A a student

B a teacher

C a principal

D a mom

2. Which title best fits the text?

A A Bell at Three

B Journals Are Fun

C Break Time at Recess

D A Busy School Day

3. What is the suffix in *independently*?

A *in–*

B *–ly*

C *–dent–*

D *–dependently*

4. Which subject is **not** taught before lunch?

A reading

B social studies

C writing

D math

NAME:_____ DATE:_____

DIRECTIONS Read the text and then answer the questions.

Chris works at the library. She is a librarian. Chris helps people find books. One day, a young girl came to the library. She wanted to know where she could find reference materials. She was trying to write a report for school. Chris helped the girl.

1. ☺ ☹

2. ☺ ☹

1. What does the girl need to find at the library?

(A) reference materials

(B) a research topic

(C) her mom

(D) books on cats

3. Which has the same root word as *reference*?

(A) reform

(B) referred

(C) reflect

(D) defer

3. ☺ ☹

4. ☺ ☹

____ / 4
Total

2. What does the text tell you about the work that librarians do?

(A) They know a lot of facts about a lot of different topics.

(B) They shelve books only in the mornings.

(C) They help people find information they are looking for.

(D) They help students get good grades on projects.

4. Which word means the same thing as *helps*?

(A) tells

(B) clues

(C) answers

(D) assists

NAME: _____ DATE: _____

A Difficult Assignment

Sara knew this day was going to come. She had been dreading it for two weeks. It started after her teacher explained the project. It was an oral report for science.

Sara loved science more than any other subject. She always checked out science books at the library. She was interested in a lot of science topics. Space and geology were her favorites. The report was going to be the easy part. The oral presentation was another story. Thinking about it kept her awake at night.

Sara feared speaking in public. It made her nervous and quiet. Her mouth would feel dry. Her hands would get clammy. Being in front of people was just plain scary.

This time, her mom tried to help. She gave Sara a few tips. First, Sara imagined her presentation. She pictured herself standing in front of the group and not being scared. Then, Sara practiced her presentation. A mirror was a big help. She even used her family as an audience. Then she got a good rest the night before. She woke up on the report day and ate a healthy breakfast.

Sara was ready. She had taken her mom's advice. She was prepared and rested. She imagined herself succeeding. It was time to go. Sara got up in front of her class. She gave her speech, and then it was over. She was thrilled! She had survived!

Her mom's plan worked. All it took was a little practice and a good attitude. She wasn't afraid of speaking in front of the class now. She knew she could do it!

NAME:_____ DATE:_____

DIRECTIONS Read "A Difficult Assignment" and then answer the questions.

1. Who might make a connection to the text?

(A) a student who has to go to the principal's office

(B) an author who is writing a story

(C) a bike rider who forgets to wear a helmet

(D) a dancer who is anxious before a show

2. What does Sara's mom give her?

(A) some tips

(B) some taps

(C) some tops

(D) some rips

3. How do Sara's hands feel when she gets nervous?

(A) clapping

(B) clamping

(C) clammy

(D) clumsy

4. What is the problem?

(A) Sara practiced her presentation.

(B) Sara did not complete an assignment correctly.

(C) Sara obeyed her mom.

(D) Sara was nervous about her presentation.

5. Which best summarizes the text?

(A) Sara was nervous about an oral report, but she took her mom's advice and did a great job.

(B) Sara was too nervous to study any other subject besides science.

(C) Sara's mom was very disappointed in Sara's work, so she took over and made things better.

(D) Sara's teacher assigned an oral report and Sara couldn't sleep.

1. ☺ ☹
2. ☺ ☹
3. ☺ ☹
4. ☺ ☹
5. ☺ ☹

___/5
Total

NAME: _____ **DATE:** _____

 Reread the text "A Difficult Assignment."

 Think about all the ways that Sara prepares herself for her presentation.

 Write about a time when you have been scared to do something. What have you done to get over your fear?

_____

_____

_____

_____

_____

_____

_____

_____

_____

#50923—180 Days of Reading for Second Grade   © Shell Education

NAME:_____ DATE:_____

DIRECTIONS Read the text and then answer the questions.

SCORE

Sleeping in space can be tricky. There is no gravity, so astronauts can float around in space. Yet crew members still have to sleep. The space station has private rooms for sleeping. The crew members are anchored to their beds.

1. ☺ ☹

2. ☺ ☹

3. ☺ ☹

4. ☺ ☹

____ / 4
Total

1. What is the text mostly about?

(A) space

(B) sleeping in space

(C) sleeping

(D) the space station

2. How do astronauts sleep in space?

(A) They are attached to a bed.

(B) They float around.

(C) They don't sleep.

(D) They all sleep in the same room.

3. Which word has the same suffix as *sleeping*?

(A) ping

(B) sleet

(C) string

(D) talking

4. Which is another meaning of *anchored*?

(A) floated

(B) attached

(C) tucked in

(D) glued

NAME:_____ DATE:_____

SCORE

1. ☺ ☹

2. ☺ ☹

3. ☺ ☹

4. ☺ ☹

____/4
Total

DIRECTIONS Read the text and then answer the questions.

A *comet* is a small solar-system body. A comet is a mix of ice, dust, and small rocks. It has a long tail made up of gas and dust particles. It can have a fuzzy outline called a *coma*. This happens when the comet gets close to the sun. Halley's Comet might be the most famous. It can be seen from Earth about every seventy-six years.

1. What is this text mostly about?

A Halley's Comet

B comets

C the solar system

D the sun

3. Which is a compound word?

A comet

B solar

C outline

D fuzzy

2. When does a comet have a fuzzy outline?

A when it explodes

B when it gets close to the sun

C every seventy-six years

D Only Halley's comet has a fuzzy outline.

4. What does *tail* mean in this text?

A back of a coin

B rear part of an animal's body

C end

D stream of gas and dust particles

NAME:_____ DATE:_____

DIRECTIONS Read the text and then answer the questions.

There used to be nine planets in the solar system. Pluto was the ninth planet. Today, Pluto is not called a planet. It is called a *dwarf planet*. It still orbits the sun like the eight planets, but it is smaller.

1. 😊 😐

2. 😊 😐

1. What does this text tell you about Pluto?

(A) Pluto used to be called a planet, and now it is called a dwarf planet.

(B) Pluto is not a dwarf planet.

(C) Pluto orbits the moon.

(D) Pluto is the largest dwarf planet.

2. What makes Pluto similar to the eight planets?

(A) It is far away.

(B) It is cold there.

(C) It orbits the sun.

(D) It is very small.

3. Which is a proper noun?

(A) planets

(B) Pluto

(C) today

(D) there

3. 😊 😐

4. 😊 😐

4. What does *orbits mean*?

(A) blocks

(B) revolves around

(C) covers

(D) shrinks

____ / 4
Total

NAME:_____ DATE:_____

Inside the Space Station

The International Space Station is like a city in space. People from sixteen different countries helped build it. Astronauts live there. They study space. They want to know how humans can live away from Earth.

A crew stays on the space station at all times. The crew rotates. Up to six people can be there at once. This gives many astronauts a turn to visit.

Crew members eat there. They have no refrigerator and only a food warmer for cans. Astronauts used to eat only freeze-dried food. They would add water and have a meal. Now, their meals look more like what we eat on Earth. They keep food on a special tray that keeps the food from floating away.

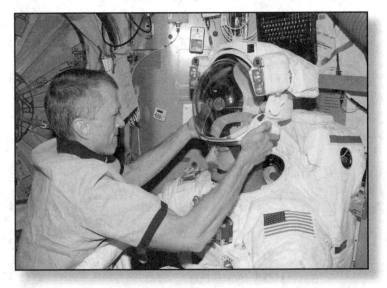

astronauts in the International Space Station

Astronauts need to stay healthy on the space station. They work hard while they are up there. Rest is very important. Crew members have a private place to sleep. Exercise is important, too. Muscles and bones grow weak in space. Astronauts have to stay fit. They may use equipment to make sure their bodies stay healthy.

Life on the space station sure is interesting!

NAME:_____ **DATE:**_____

SCORE

DIRECTIONS Read "Inside the Space Station" and then answer the questions.

1. Which is similar to the life explained in the text?

(A) moving to a new house

(B) getting used to eating food with water

(C) getting used to living in a new country

(D) looking at the stars in the night sky

2. What is a group of astronauts called?

(A) a crow

(B) a crew

(C) a craw

(D) a chew

3. Which definition of *fit* is used in the fourth paragraph?

(A) appropriate

(B) tantrum

(C) correct size

(D) strong and healthy

4. Which topic is **not** covered about life on the space station?

(A) sleeping on the space station

(B) exercising on the space station

(C) eating on the space station

(D) chores on the space station

5. Which gives the best summary of the text?

(A) The space station is like a city in space, and astronauts work hard to learn about life there.

(B) The space station was built by people from around the world.

(C) Astronauts can eat regular food on the space station.

(D) Astronauts must exercise.

1. ☺ ☹
2. ☺ ☹
3. ☺ ☹
4. ☺ ☹
5. ☺ ☹

___ / 5
Total

NAME:_____ DATE:_____

 Reread the text "Inside the Space Station."

 Think about what life sounds like on the space station.

✏️ **Write about** whether you would want to live on the space station. Tell why or why not.

_____

_____

_____

_____

_____

_____

_____

_____

_____

_____

_____

NAME:_____ DATE:_____

DIRECTIONS Read the text and then answer the questions.

   The troll under the bridge was scary. The animals did not want to cross over because they were afraid. The troll was always saying he would eat them. One day, a brave billy goat crossed the bridge. He was very surprised when nothing happened. Then he heard cries coming from below. The troll was sad. He was lonesome and wanted to make some friends. He had changed his ways and did not want to scare others anymore.

1. ☺ ☻

2. ☺ ☻

3. ☺ ☻

4. ☺ ☻

____ / 4
Total

1. What is the main idea?

(A) The bridge is scary.

(B) A brave billy goat discovers that the troll is sad.

(C) The troll scares everyone.

(D) The troll cries.

2. What lesson does this text teach?

(A) Don't cross bridges.

(B) You don't always know what someone else is feeling.

(C) Trolls are always mean.

(D) Someone who cries must be pretty sad.

3. Which is the compound word in the text?

(A) crossed

(B) others

(C) changed

(D) anymore

4. What does the word *ways* mean in the last sentence?

(A) distance

(B) direction

(C) behavior

(D) voice

NAME:_____ **DATE:**_____

1. ☺ ☹

2. ☺ ☹

3. ☺ ☹

4. ☺ ☹

___ / 4
Total

DIRECTIONS Read the text and then answer the questions.

"Bleck!" cried the princess. "Who would ever kiss a frog? They are the most disgusting animals. I would never even get near one."

"Well, that is not very nice," said the frog. "I would have hoped you would be more cordial than that. I really am a nice creature. I am definitely not as slimy as you think. You have upset me."

1. How many characters are in the text?

(A) one character

(B) two characters

(C) three characters

(D) four characters

2. How do the characters feel about each other?

(A) The princess is angry and the frog is sad.

(B) The princess is confused and the frog is snobby.

(C) The princess and the frog are disgusted by each other.

(D) The princess is disgusted and the frog is upset.

3. What is the suffix in *definitely*?

(A) *de–*

(B) *–ly*

(C) *–finitely*

(D) define

4. What does the word *cordial* mean in the text?

(A) quiet

(B) honest

(C) friendly

(D) scared

NAME: _____ **DATE:** _____

DIRECTIONS Read the text and then answer the questions.

The horses began to feel nervous. The clock was about to strike midnight. They knew what had happened before. The clock strikes. Then the night is over. The horses go back to being the small mice they were before. No more fancy carriages to pull. No more elegant balls to visit.

1. Which fairy tale does the text sound like?

(A) "Jack and the Beanstalk"

(B) "Cinderella"

(C) "Snow White and the Seven Dwarfs"

(D) "Rumpelstiltskin"

2. Why are the horses feeling nervous?

(A) They know the fancy ball is about to start.

(B) They know they will change back into mice.

(C) They know the carriage is about to crash.

(D) They know they are about to change into unicorns.

3. Which word has the same root as *happened*?

(A) napping

(B) happy

(C) unhappy

(D) happening

4. What does it mean for a clock to *strike midnight*?

(A) sound an alarm

(B) turn off when it is midnight

(C) make a sound when it is midnight

(D) turn back on at midnight

NAME:_____   DATE:_____

Once Upon a Time

Once upon a time, an elf began a very special journey. He was trying to get to the king's castle because he had an important gift to bring to the queen.

There was a problem. No one trusted the elf because he was naughty and annoying. He played tricks on people all the time, so no one knew when to trust him.

When he arrived at the castle gates, the guards tried to turn the elf away. The elf used his magic to get past them. The king and queen were quite startled to see the elf coming into their living room.

"What are you doing here?" the king demanded.

"I have something for the queen. I found it in the woods," the elf replied.

"Is this another one of your tricks?" the queen asked.

"No, it is not. When I found this, I knew I had to return it to Your Majesty." The elf opened his satchel and took out a beautiful crown. It belonged to the queen. She had lost it on one of her trips around the kingdom. She could not believe it. Why would this naughty elf do such a good deed?

"I knew it was yours, and I knew you would want it back. I may play tricks on people, but I am no thief!"

From that day forward, people in the kingdom began to see the elf in a new way. The king and queen were forever grateful to him. They knew he was a good elf who could be trusted.

NAME:_____ DATE:_____

DIRECTIONS Read "Once Upon a Time" and then answer the questions.

SCORE

1. Which shows a connection to the text?

(A) I walked all the way to the garden to pick a flower for my friend.

(B) I saw a movie that had elves in it.

(C) I found my sister's favorite necklace but gave it back to her.

(D) I pretend to use magic with my best friends.

2. What does the elf return?

(A) a crown

(B) a crow

(C) a clown

(D) a crop

3. Which is **not** another word for *satchel*?

(A) bag

(B) purse

(C) horse

(D) sack

4. How does the queen's opinion of the elf change?

(A) She distrusted him, then appreciated him.

(B) She liked him, then became angry at him.

(C) She distrusted him, then distrusted him more.

(D) She hated him, then distrusted him.

5. Which title is the best summary of the text?

(A) A Mystery in the Woods

(B) Silliness at the Castle

(C) A Few Mean Knights

(D) A Changing Elf

1. ☺ ☺

2. ☺ ☺

3. ☺ ☺

4. ☺ ☺

5. ☺ ☺

___ / 5

Total

SCORE

___/4

NAME: _____ **DATE:** _____

Reread the text "Once Upon a Time."

Think about how people's opinions of the elf changed in the text.

Write about a time when you changed your mind about something or someone.

_____

_____

_____

_____

_____

_____

_____

_____

_____

_____

_____

#50923—*180 Days of Reading for Second Grade*

NAME:_____ DATE:_____

DIRECTIONS Read the text and then answer the questions.

> An earthquake shakes the ground. The earth far below our feet moves. Earthquakes can be a quick jolt. They can be a rolling motion. They can last a second or longer. Earthquakes surprise people when they happen. It is important to stay calm and to get to a safe place.

1. ☺ ☺

2. ☺ ☺

3. ☺ ☺

4. ☺ ☺

1. What is this text mostly about?

- (A) shocks
- (B) earthquakes
- (C) rolling motions
- (D) staying calm

3. Which word has the same suffix as *rolling*?

- (A) ball
- (B) rolled
- (C) making
- (D) ring

____ / 4

Total

2. How long does an earthquake last?

- (A) one second
- (B) many seconds
- (C) it varies
- (D) one minute

4. Which words are similar in meaning?

- (A) *calm* and *quick*
- (B) *jolt* and *shake*
- (C) *surprise* and *motion*
- (D) *place* and *safe*

NAME:_____ DATE:_____

DIRECTIONS Read the text and then answer the questions.

Scientists try to learn from storms. They collect data. They want to be able to predict when a storm is coming. A hurricane is one example. Scientists study wind patterns. They watch how a storm changes. They observe rain levels. They want to give people enough time to get to a safe place.

1. What is the main idea?

(A) Scientists study and observe storms.

(B) Scientists collect data on storms.

(C) Scientists watch rain levels.

(D) Scientists learn from storms so they can give people warning.

2. Why do scientists want to predict storms?

(A) to give people accurate data

(B) to give people time to get somewhere safe

(C) to know when to get the best readings

(D) to know where the storm is headed

3. Which suffix could be added to the root word *come*?

(A) –er

(B) –ed

(C) –s

(D) –ion

4. What do people often try to *predict*?

(A) what direction a car will turn

(B) what happens next in a book

(C) what is being served for dinner

(D) what a birthday party will be like

NAME:_____ **DATE:**_____

DIRECTIONS Read the text and then answer the questions.

It is important to prepare for disasters. Think about where you live. What happens there? Do you see tornadoes? Are hurricanes common? Is there risk of an earthquake? Prepare for what you may face one day. Better to be safe than sorry!

1. ☺ ☺

2. ☺ ☺

3. ☺ ☺

4. ☺ ☺

1. What word sums up the main idea?

(A) tornadoes

(B) risk

(C) prepare

(D) safe

3. Which suffix does **not** work with the root word *prepare*?

(A) –ed

(B) –ing

(C) –ly

(D) –s

_____ / 4
Total

2. What does the text recommend?

(A) Prepare yourself for a tornado.

(B) Prepare yourself for a hurricane.

(C) Prepare yourself for the natural disasters that are most common in your area.

(D) Prepare yourself for an earthquake.

4. What is another way to say *Better to be safe than sorry*?

(A) It is better to be safe and say sorry.

(B) Stay safe in a disaster by leaving your home.

(C) Use a safe so your things are not stolen.

(D) It is better to prepare and be ready than not to prepare and regret it.

NAME:_____ DATE:_____

Natural Disasters

A natural disaster is often a sudden event. It is usually intense. It has extreme results. It is caused by natural factors. It might start with rain or heavy winds. A volcano erupts. The Earth shakes. A tsunami hits the coast. These are all natural disasters.

Natural disasters can happen anywhere. They can occur at any time. Some areas are prone to big storms. Other areas have tornadoes. Tsunamis are a worry for people who live by the ocean. It all depends on where you live.

building after a natural disaster

Disasters are scary. They often hurt or kill people. They can cause a lot of damage. Buildings can be destroyed. Entire towns can be ruined.

One way to handle a disaster is to plan ahead. Planning can keep us safe. It also gives us peace of mind. We know we are ready. Other people help us prepare. Some areas have warnings. They tell people to evacuate to a safe place. They let people know when a big disaster may be on the way. Other disasters happen too quickly. An earthquake can surprise you. There is no warning. An earthquake kit can help you after the event.

Where do you live? What happens in your town or city? Think ahead. Find out what you need. Make a plan with your family. Be ready! That is the best you can do.

NAME:_____ DATE:_____

DIRECTIONS Read "Natural Disasters" and then answer the questions.

1. Who might make a connection to the text?

(A) a teacher who reads about tsunamis

(B) a mother who follows weather forecasts

(C) a boy who likes to watch waves in a storm

(D) a girl who has lived through a hurricane by evacuating

2. Before a natural disaster occurs,

(A) plane ahead.

(B) plan ahead.

(C) pan ahead.

(D) plot ahead.

3. What does the word *prone* mean?

(A) will occur

(B) likely to occur

(C) won't occur

(D) cannot occur

4. Which is the main idea of this text?

(A) disaster predicting

(B) disaster reporting

(C) disaster preparedness

(D) disaster warnings

5. Which gives the best summary of the text?

(A) Hurricanes occur only in certain places.

(B) Preparing for a tornado takes a lot of time.

(C) Preparing for a natural disaster is a smart thing to do.

(D) People far from the coast don't need to worry about tsunamis.

1.

2.

3.

4.

5.

____ / 5
Total

NAME:_____ DATE:_____

SCORE

___/4

Reread the text "Natural Disasters."

Think about your experiences with natural disasters.

Write about how you are prepared for a natural disaster.

_____

_____

_____

_____

_____

_____

_____

_____

_____

_____

_____

_____

NAME:_____ **DATE:**_____

DIRECTIONS Read the text and then answer the questions.

> Paul could not wait for reading time. His teacher had been reading fables. Paul loved them. They were fictional stories. The characters could be like humans. They could be animals or plants. They could be objects or pretend creatures. Each fable taught a lesson, or a moral. Paul thought a lot about each fable's moral.

1. ☺ ☺

2. ☺ ☺

3. ☺ ☺

4. ☺ ☺

____ / 4

Total

1. What makes fable characters interesting?

(A) They have to be talking animals.

(B) They can be make-believe, but can act like people.

(C) The plants and animals don't get along.

(D) They are nonfictional.

2. What does the text **not** say about fables?

(A) They have a moral.

(B) They are fictional stories.

(C) They have pretend creatures with human qualities.

(D) They have been exaggerated over time.

3. How many syllables are in the word *character*?

(A) five syllables

(B) two syllables

(C) three syllables

(D) four syllables

4. Which is another word for *moral*?

(A) problem

(B) character

(C) lesson

(D) ending

NAME: _____ **DATE:** _____

DIRECTIONS Read the text and then answer the questions.

Emma and Parker were running on the track. Emma ran so fast that she was soon out of energy. Parker took his time and jogged slowly. He kept going. He ran farther than Emma. Emma said, "We are just like the tortoise and the hare!" That made Parker laugh very hard.

1. Who runs farther on the track?

(A) Parker

(B) Emma

(C) They tied.

(D) They both stopped.

2. How does Emma's run compare to Parker's?

(A) Parker ran faster, while Emma jogged slower.

(B) Emma ran faster and won the race.

(C) Emma ran faster, but Parker ran farther.

(D) Parker ran faster, but Emma ran farther.

3. How is the word *running* divided into syllables?

(A) runn-ing

(B) ru-nning

(C) runnin-g

(D) run-ning

4. What is Emma talking about when she says they are like *the tortoise and the hare*?

(A) a television show

(B) two stuffed animals

(C) a fable

(D) a song

NAME:_____ DATE:_____

DIRECTIONS Read the text and then answer the questions.

Jesse loved to jump on his bed, but this always made his mom worry about him getting hurt. She told him not to jump on the bed, but he did it anyway. One day, Jesse lost his balance, fell off the bed, and hit his head. He had to get stitches. His mom was very upset. She hoped that he had learned a lesson.

1. 😊 😐

2. 😊 😐

3. 😊 😐

4. 😊 😐

1. What happens after Jesse loses his balance?

(A) He falls off the bed.

(B) He gets stitches.

(C) His mother is upset.

(D) He jumps on the bed again.

2. What is the text mostly about?

(A) Jesse not listening to his mom and getting hurt

(B) Jesse getting stitches

(C) Jesse arguing with his mom

(D) Jesse losing his balance

3. Which word has two syllables?

(A) balance

(B) hoped

(C) jump

(D) made

4. Which two words are similar in meaning?

(A) *worry* and *jump*

(B) *hoped* and *loved*

(C) *upset* and *worry*

(D) *lost* and *fell*

____ / 4
Total

NAME:_____ DATE:_____

The Ant and the Grasshopper

One summer day in a field, a grasshopper was hopping about. He was singing and chirping. An ant passed by. He was trying to carry an ear of corn he was taking to the anthill.

The grasshopper invited the ant to sit and chat with him. He wanted a singing partner. But the ant refused, saying, "I'm storing up food for winter." Then the ant asked the grasshopper, "Why don't you do the same?"

"Oh dear! Why bother about winter?" said the grasshopper. "We have got enough food right now."

So the ant went on its way and continued its hard work. Soon the weather turned cold. All the food lying in the field was covered with snow. Even the grasshopper could not dig through it. The grasshopper found himself starving. He saw the ants distributing corn and grain from storage. He begged them for something to eat.

"What? You have not stored anything away for the winter? What were you doing all summer?" the ants asked.

"I was too busy playing music. Before I knew it, summer was over," complained the grasshopper.

The ants shook their heads. They turned their backs on the grasshopper. Then they went on with their work.

The moral is: There is a time for work and a time for play.

NAME:_____ **DATE:**_____

DIRECTIONS   Read "The Ant and the Grasshopper" and then answer the questions.

1. Who might make a connection to the text?

(A) a person who hates snow

(B) a person who likes to sing

(C) a person who picks on smaller people

(D) a person who likes to put chores off until later

2. What does the food have on it when the weather turns cold?

(A) slow

(B) show

(C) snow

(D) snew

3. Which definition of *ear* is used in the text?

(A) talent

(B) part of a body

(C) listen

(D) part of a corn plant

4. What is the grasshopper's mistake?

(A) He loves to sing.

(B) He is mean to the ants.

(C) He doesn't prepare ahead of time.

(D) He hates summer.

5. What does the grasshopper learn?

(A) that music can distract you

(B) that ants are not very giving

(C) that winter is cold

(D) that playing for too long and avoiding work is a bad idea

1. ☺ ☺

2. ☺ ☺

3. ☺ ☺

4. ☺ ☺

5. ☺ ☺

___ / 5

Total

NAME: _____ **DATE:** _____

Reread the text "The Ant and the Grasshopper."

Think about how the ants treat the grasshopper.

Write about what you think might happen if the ants give the grasshopper some food in the winter. Continue the story on the lines below, writing a new ending.

_____

_____

_____

_____

_____

_____

_____

_____

_____

_____

_____

NAME:_____ DATE:_____

DIRECTIONS Read the text and then answer the questions.

Plants and animals need water to survive. In some places, there is a lot of rain. In other places, the climate is very dry. A *drought* (drout) is a long period of dry weather that can be harmful to people. If plants cannot grow, then food is not made. Droughts can last for months or years.

1. ☺ 😐

2. ☺ 😐

3. ☺ 😐

4. ☺ 😐

____ / 4
Total

1. Which statement about water is true?

(A) Plants and animals need water.

(B) People need less water than plants.

(C) Too much water can cause a drought.

(D) Water is not necessary for plants to grow.

2. What happens if plants do not grow?

(A) A drought gets worse.

(B) The climate will become drier.

(C) Food is not made.

(D) The drought will end.

3. What is the root word in *harmful*?

(A) ful

(B) armful

(C) arm

(D) harm

4. Which word means almost the same as *climate*?

(A) survive

(B) plant

(C) weather

(D) water

NAME:_____ DATE:_____

DIRECTIONS Read the text and then answer the questions.

1. ☺ ☺

2. ☺ ☺

> Water is unique. It has special properties. Water can be a solid, a liquid, or a gas. No other substance can do that. Water can be frozen. Freezing it changes water to ice. Ice can melt. This changes water back to a liquid. Then the water can be heated. It becomes a gas.

3. ☺ ☺

4. ☺ ☺

___ / 4
Total

1. What is the main idea?

(A) Water becomes a gas when it is heated.

(B) Water becomes a liquid when it melts.

(C) Water is unique because it can be a solid, a liquid, or a gas.

(D) Ice is water as a solid.

2. What happens when water freezes?

(A) It changes to ice.

(B) It changes to a gas.

(C) It becomes unique.

(D) It changes to a liquid.

3. Which words have the same vowel sound?

(A) *melt* and *gas*

(B) *freezing* and *heated*

(C) *unique* and *liquid*

(D) *changes* and *water*

4. What do you know about the meaning of the word *unique* by reading this text?

(A) It is about heating and freezing something.

(B) It describes a liquid.

(C) It describes something related to water.

(D) It describes something that is one-of-a-kind.

NAME:_____ **DATE:**_____

Read the text and then answer
the questions.

Large pieces of ice are melting on Earth right now. They are called *ice caps*. These are like mountains of ice. The melted ice causes a lot of problems. It raises the water levels in our oceans. The higher water levels cause flooding. Why are the ice caps melting? Because our planet is getting warmer and warmer each year.

1. ☺ ☺

2. ☺ ☺

3. ☺ ☺

4. ☺ ☺

____ / 4
Total

1. What is causing the ice caps to melt?

Ⓐ The ocean levels are rising.

Ⓑ The planet is getting warmer.

Ⓒ flooding

Ⓓ The mountains of ice are freezing.

2. What are ice caps?

Ⓐ flooding

Ⓑ frozen oceans

Ⓒ mountains of ice

Ⓓ ice cubes

3. Which suffix could be added to the root word *melt*?

Ⓐ *–less*

Ⓑ *–er*

Ⓒ *–s*

Ⓓ *–tion*

4. Which of the following could cause *flooding*?

Ⓐ high water levels

Ⓑ a drought

Ⓒ an earthquake

Ⓓ a full moon

NAME:_____ DATE:_____

The Water Cycle

There is only so much water on Earth. New water is not being made anywhere. Instead, water is recycled over and over. The water from a lake comes from the rain in a cloud. That cloud is made up of water that came from the lake. This process is called the *water cycle*.

The water cycle has four parts. First, water comes down from the sky. This is called *precipitation* (pri-sip-i-TEY-shuhn). It might be rain or hail. It could be snow or sleet, too. The water comes from clouds. It falls to the ground and collects in puddles. It also goes into oceans, lakes, and rivers. This is called *collection*.

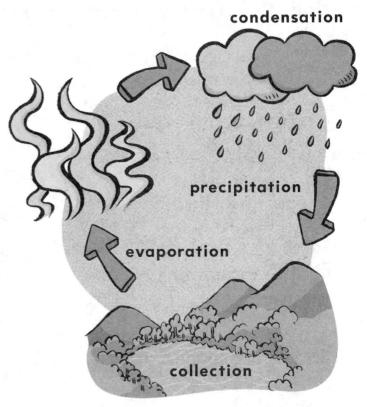

condensation

precipitation

evaporation

collection

Then the sun heats the water in the oceans, lakes, and rivers. It turns the water into a gas. The *vapor* (VEY-per), or steam, goes into the air. This is called *evaporation* (ih-vap-uh-REY-shuhn).

When the water goes into the air, it gets cold. Finally, the water changes back into clouds. This is called *condensation* (kon-den-SEY-shuhn). The clouds gather more and more water. They get heavy. What happens next? It rains! The water cycle starts all over again.

NAME:_____ **DATE:**_____

DIRECTIONS Read "The Water Cycle" and then answer the questions.

1. Which is **not** a real-world example of the water cycle?

(A) the summer sun warming a lake

(B) snow melting

(C) drinking a glass of water

(D) clouds about to burst with rain

2. Water gathered on the ground and in oceans and lakes is called

(A) convection.

(B) connection.

(C) collection.

(D) correction.

3. What is the gas form of water called?

(A) vapor

(B) hail

(C) sleet

(D) snow

4. What is the correct order of the water cycle?

(A) precipitation, collection, evaporation, condensation

(B) collection, precipitation, condensation, evaporation

(C) precipitation, evaporation, condensation, collection

(D) condensation, precipitation, evaporation, collection

5. What is the main idea?

(A) Water can fall as rain, snow, sleet, or hail.

(B) Water is recycled over and over.

(C) There is less water on Earth now than there was 100 years ago.

(D) It is not safe to drink water from a lake or ocean.

1. ☺ ☹

2. ☺ ☹

3. ☺ ☹

4. ☺ ☹

5. ☺ ☹

____ / 5
Total

NAME:_____ DATE:_____

SCORE

___/4

Reread the text "The Water Cycle."

Think about how the water cycle is a process that follows a certain order.

Write about and describe the water cycle to someone who is learning about it for the first time. Explain it in the correct order.

_____

_____

_____

_____

_____

_____

_____

_____

_____

_____

_____

NAME: _____ **DATE:** _____

DIRECTIONS Read the text and then answer the questions.

The music kept playing. The players walked in a circle. Each person tried to find a chair when the music stopped. With each round, one of the chairs disappeared. That meant that someone was always left out with nowhere to sit. Better move fast! The music might stop any second!

1. 😊 😐

2. 😊 😐

3. 😊 😐

4. 😊 😐

___ / 4
Total

1. What happens with each round?

Ⓐ The chairs move.

Ⓑ The music speeds up.

Ⓒ One chair is taken away.

Ⓓ The chairs are turned over.

2. What is the text mostly about?

Ⓐ a game

Ⓑ exercising

Ⓒ a music class

Ⓓ a lesson

3. How many syllables are in the word *nowhere*?

Ⓐ one syllable

Ⓑ two syllables

Ⓒ three syllables

Ⓓ four syllables

4. Which meaning of the word *round* is used in the text?

Ⓐ plump

Ⓑ complete

Ⓒ circular

Ⓓ stage of a game

NAME: _____ **DATE:** _____

SCORE

1. ☺ ☹

2. ☺ ☹

3. ☺ ☹

4. ☺ ☹

___ / 4
Total

DIRECTIONS Read the text and then answer the questions.

Suki thought that hobbies were fun. She could try something new anytime. It helped her learn about what she liked. Art and soccer were her favorites. She did not like piano lessons. Collecting stamps was boring. Martial arts were interesting to her. Maybe she should take a class. Then she could decide if she liked it.

1. Why does Suki think that hobbies are fun?

Ⓐ Because she only enjoys art and soccer

Ⓑ Because she could try new things to see what she liked

Ⓒ Because she is bored at school

Ⓓ Because you never change your hobbies

2. What is the text mostly about?

Ⓐ hobbies

Ⓑ collecting stamps

Ⓒ taking classes

Ⓓ lessons

3. How would the word *interesting* be divided into syllables?

Ⓐ inter-est-ing

Ⓑ in-ter-esting

Ⓒ in-terest-ing

Ⓓ in-ter-est-ing

4. What is an example of *martial arts*?

Ⓐ painting

Ⓑ karate

Ⓒ ceramics

Ⓓ marching

NAME:_____ **DATE:**_____

DIRECTIONS Read the text and then answer the questions.

Summer vacation was finally here! There were endless days to play, be outside, and have fun in the sun. The days were long. There was no homework to do or bells to follow. The first week was perfect. But the second week was difficult. What was there to do? It was time to find a new activity to enjoy!

1. 😊 😐

2. 😊 😐

3. 😊 😐

4. 😊 😐

____ / 4
Total

1. What happens during the second week of summer?

(A) The narrator is tired.

(B) The narrator becomes bored.

(C) The narrator goes swimming.

(D) The narrator has homework.

2. What does the text tell you about summer?

(A) It goes by fast.

(B) It is free time without school schedules.

(C) It is lazy.

(D) It is warm.

3. How many syllables are in the word *activity*?

(A) two syllables

(B) three syllables

(C) four syllables

(D) five syllables

4. Which two words are similar in meaning?

(A) *fun* and *enjoy*

(B) *new* and *outside*

(C) *follow* and *activity*

(D) *first* and *second*

NAME:_____ DATE:_____

A New Hobby

The school band had sent home a notice to parents. They were looking for new students to join. The band teacher was excited for the band to grow. He promised to help students who had never played before.

José wanted to play an instrument. He had loved music his entire life. He loved singing and dancing. He knew a little bit about reading music. Now he was ready to join the band.

José was torn. He could not decide which instrument to learn how to play. His brother played the drums. His friend played the tuba. His neighbor played the clarinet. He thought those instruments were fun. Which one was the right one for him? José went to talk to the teacher, Mr. Riley. He was nervous. He hoped Mr. Riley would help him.

Mr. Riley told José that many students struggle to pick an instrument. It is a big decision. Band members spend a lot of time practicing and playing. They talked about the good and bad things about each choice. The tuba was heavy, but unique. The drums were not easy to move around, but they were fun to play. The clarinet was challenging, but had a great sound. In the end, José picked the saxophone! He joined the band. He loved every minute of learning about music.

 #50923—180 Days of Reading for Second Grade

NAME:_____ **DATE:**_____

SCORE

DIRECTIONS Read "A New Hobby" and then answer the questions.

1. Who might make a connection to the text?

(A) a kid who dislikes music

(B) a person who is choosing a second language to learn

(C) a drummer who likes to watch music videos

(D) a music shop owner who sells instruments

2. What is José going to join?

(A) the bond

(B) the bind

(C) the bend

(D) the band

3. What does the word *grow* mean in the first paragraph?

(A) get bigger

(B) get taller

(C) raise crops

(D) breed

4. What is the problem?

(A) José doesn't like music.

(B) José doesn't want to join the band.

(C) José doesn't know which instrument to play.

(D) José didn't know where the band room is.

5. Which gives the best summary of the story?

(A) José likes the clarinet, but settles for the tuba.

(B) José does not agree with the band teacher and does his own thing.

(C) José is nervous to pick an instrument and join the band, but he works through it and has a great time.

(D) José's school band is in danger of being cancelled, and then he decides to join.

1. ☺ ☹

2. ☺ ☹

3. ☺ ☹

4. ☺ ☹

5. ☺ ☹

___ / 5
Total

NAME:_____ DATE:_____

 Reread the text "A New Hobby."

 Think about how José works hard to learn something new.

 Write about a time when you worked hard to learn something new.

_____

_____

_____

_____

_____

_____

_____

_____

_____

_____

_____

_____

_____

_____

NAME: _____ **DATE:** _____

DIRECTIONS Read the text and then answer the questions.

Fall is special. It is a unique season. It's when harvest festivals occur. Harvest time is a time to gather. People enjoy the harvest. They give thanks for the food. They prepare for the long winter.

1. ☺ ☺

2. ☺ ☺

3. ☺ ☺

4. ☺ ☺

___ / 4
Total

1. According to the text, what makes fall special?

(A) harvest festivals

(B) a long winter that comes after

(C) the end of summer

(D) It is also called autumn.

2. What is **not** done to celebrate the harvest?

(A) gathering

(B) preparing for the winter

(C) eating the entire harvest

(D) giving thanks

3. What does the contraction *it's* mean?

(A) its is

(B) it was

(C) it is

(D) it us

4. What does it mean to *give thanks*?

(A) make a Thanksgiving meal

(B) celebrate with a large party

(C) give a thank-you letter

(D) feel thankful

NAME:_____ DATE:_____

DIRECTIONS Read the text and then answer the questions.

1. ☺ ☹

   Farmers pay close attention to weather. Most follow the forecast. They watch for rain. They know if snow's coming. They want to know about storms. Floods and droughts are the most serious. They can ruin an entire crop. A farmer's life will always be affected by weather.

2. ☺ ☹

3. ☺ ☹

4. ☺ ☹

1. How are farmers and weather related?

- (A) A farmer's crop is always ruined by weather.
- (B) A farmer's crop is always determined by weather.
- (C) A farmer's crop only grows in good weather.
- (D) A farmer can always predict the weather.

____/4
Total

2. What is the most serious weather that farmers watch for?

- (A) rain
- (B) floods and droughts
- (C) snow
- (D) storms

3. Which suffix can be added to the root word *serious*?

- (A) *–ly*
- (B) *–tion*
- (C) *–er*
- (D) *–ed*

4. What is a weather *forecast*?

- (A) a report
- (B) a prediction
- (C) a test
- (D) a measurement

NAME:_____ DATE:_____

DIRECTIONS Read the text and then answer the questions.

Schools want to serve good food. A healthy diet is important. It is about good nutrition. Lunchrooms now have more fruits and vegetables. They do not offer junk food. This also means no soda or juice. Most parents are happy with this new idea.

1. Why should schools serve healthy food?

(A) because it is faster to make

(B) because it costs less

(C) because all kids like fruits and vegetables

(D) because good nutrition is important for young kids

2. What is considered junk food?

(A) apples

(B) cheese

(C) soda

(D) milk

3. Which word from the text **cannot** have an –s suffix?

(A) food

(B) healthy

(C) idea

(D) fruit

4. Which food would **not** be considered part of a *healthy diet*?

(A) potato chips

(B) carrots

(C) watermelon

(D) yogurt

SCORE

1. ☺ ☹
2. ☺ ☹
3. ☺ ☹
4. ☺ ☹

___ / 4
Total

NAME: _____ **DATE:** _____

Farm to Table

The corn on your plate did not grow in a store. It grew on a farm. A farmer planted that corn seed and then helped it to grow. Ears of corn were picked from their stalks. They likely came to the store in a truck.

It is important to know where your food comes from before you eat it. Foods that can be traced to a farm, an orchard, or a ranch are often the healthiest to eat. Fruits and vegetables are some of those foods. Meat and dairy products are other examples.

Farmers and farm workers help you get the food that you need to eat. They watch over plants and animals. They tend to crops. They also milk cows and gather eggs from chickens. Without this work, there would be no food coming into the stores.

Truck drivers are part of the process, too. They bring the nutritious food from the farm to the store. This means that you do not have to travel to the farm yourself. This way, you can go to a store in town and find what you need.

Finally, the store workers organize the food. They keep it fresh. They keep some foods cold or frozen. Store workers make sure you are buying food that is still healthy to eat.

During the next meal that you eat, think about where your food comes from. Imagine who might have picked that corn. Picture the person who grew the wheat for your bread. How would you eat eggs if someone had not cared for the chickens?

NAME:_____ **DATE:**_____

DIRECTIONS Read "Farm to Table" and then answer the questions.

1. How is this important for all readers?

(A) All readers have visited a farm.

(B) All readers have milked a cow.

(C) All readers can think about where their food comes from.

(D) All readers eat healthy food.

2. Where does most of our food come from?

(A) a warm

(B) a firm

(C) a form

(D) a farm

3. Which comes from an *orchard*?

(A) milk

(B) chicken

(C) peaches

(D) pork

4. What is true about food that comes from a farm?

(A) It is always picked by a farm worker.

(B) It is usually the healthiest type of food to eat.

(C) It is old by the time it gets to your table.

(D) It travels by airplane to get to the store.

5. What does this text encourage the reader to do?

(A) to work on a farm

(B) to milk a cow

(C) to think about the people who helped get food on their table

(D) to visit a ranch

1. ☺ ☺

2. ☺ ☺

3. ☺ ☺

4. ☺ ☺

5. ☺ ☺

____ / 5
Total

NAME: _____ **DATE:** _____

 Reread the text "Farm to Table."

 Think about a food that you have eaten lately.

 Write about and describe the food. Where did it come from? How did it get to your table?

_____

_____

_____

_____

_____

_____

_____

_____

_____

_____

NAME: _____ DATE: _____

DIRECTIONS Read the text and then answer the questions.

Nina's teacher had it all wrong. The principal did, too. She was not talking during the fire drill. She was totally silent. She followed the rules. Nina's teacher must have misheard the voice. Nina thought she confused her with Jada. So Nina had to say something. She wanted to stand up for herself.

1. ☺ ☹

2. ☺ ☹

3. ☺ ☹

4. ☺ ☹

___ / 4
Total

1. Who is the main character?

(A) the principal

(B) the teacher

(C) Jada

(D) Nina

2. What is the text mostly about?

(A) Nina standing next to Jada

(B) Nina's teacher and principal being wrong

(C) Nina getting in trouble for something she didn't do

(D) Nina talking during the fire drill

3. Which suffix could be added to the root word *stand*?

(A) –ed

(B) –tion

(C) –er

(D) –ing

4. What does the author mean when she says that Nina wanted to *stand up for herself*?

(A) Nina has to walk alone.

(B) Nina has to grow taller.

(C) Nina has to stand up.

(D) Nina has to speak up about the truth.

NAME:_____ DATE:_____

DIRECTIONS Read the text and then answer the questions.

1. ☺ ☹

2. ☺ ☹

3. ☺ ☹

4. ☺ ☹

____/ 4
Total

Monica had the quietest voice. "I cannot hear you!" people would say. "Why don't you speak up?" people would ask, but Monica liked to be quiet because it helped her feel calm inside. She knew that she could speak up if she needed to. Otherwise, she was okay with being the quiet one in the class.

1. Why does Monica like to be quiet?

(A) because she has nothing to say

(B) because it helps her feel calm inside

(C) because she does not know how to speak up for herself

(D) because she is a mouse

2. What is the text mostly about?

(A) voice lessons

(B) being okay with who you are

(C) a classroom

(D) secrets

3. Which two words make the contraction *don't*?

(A) does not

(B) do not

(C) don it

(D) did not

4. What does being *calm inside* refer to in the text?

(A) feeling peaceful

(B) having a calm stomach

(C) having a quiet brain

(D) feeling cold

NAME:_____ DATE:_____

DIRECTIONS Read the text and then answer the questions.

Kevin really liked his reading buddy, Ted, who was in fifth grade. Kevin was in second grade. Their classes met each Friday. Each second-grader was paired up with a fifth-grader. They read together. Kevin had fun with Ted. He saw him on the playground. Kevin never worried that he would be teased by the older boys.

1. ☺ ☺

2. ☺ ☺

3. ☺ ☺

4. ☺ ☺

____ / 4
Total

1. Who are Kevin and Ted?

(A) reading buddies

(B) brothers

(C) classmates

(D) enemies

2. What does the text tell you about what reading buddies are?

(A) They are kids who take reading tests together.

(B) They are two kids from two different grades who read together.

(C) They are two kids who hate to read and play together.

(D) They are friends who have a reading group.

3. Which suffix could be added to the root word *pair*?

(A) –*tion*

(B) –*ly*

(C) –*ing*

(D) –*er*

4. Which word means *worried*?

(A) predicted

(B) said

(C) full

(D) concerned

NAME:_____ DATE:_____

No More Bullying

Two girls followed Sam home from school. He was walking by himself because his brother was home sick. He could hear the girls behind him. They were giggling and saying rude things. It felt like they were getting closer and closer.

Sam did not know why the girls were teasing him. He barely knew them, though one of the girls lived around the corner. Sam even thought she might be friends with his brother. Why was she being so mean to him? Sam started to walk quickly.

He rounded the corner to his street. His house was five houses away. He could see his car and his mailbox. He was so close. He began to jog.

The girls jogged after him, but then Sam surprised them when he stopped running and turned around. "Why are you following me?" he yelled. "I don't like it, and I think you are bullying me."

The girls stopped in their tracks. "Bullying?" one asked. "No, we aren't. We are just having fun."

"What you are doing is not funny to me," said Sam. "Please stop and leave me alone!"

"Okay, sorry, Sam," the girls muttered. They looked sad, but Sam was glad. He had taught them a lesson. What might seem fun can make someone else uncomfortable, and that is not okay. Sam walked into his house, hoping they would not bother him, or anyone else, again.

NAME:_____ DATE:_____

DIRECTIONS Read "No More Bullying" and then answer the questions.

1. Who might make a connection to the text?

- (A) any younger brother
- (B) anyone who has been bullied
- (C) any boy
- (D) a girl who has walked home

2. What does Sam do as he gets near home?

- (A) jig
- (B) jag
- (C) jog
- (D) jug

3. What does it mean to make someone *uncomfortable*?

- (A) make someone yell
- (B) make someone walk fast
- (C) make someone feel sad
- (D) make someone worry and feel uneasy

4. What is the problem?

- (A) Sam's brother is sick.
- (B) Sam is angry.
- (C) Sam is bothered by the girls.
- (D) Sam gets lost walking home.

5. Which gives the best summary of the text?

- (A) Sam is followed and teased on his way home.
- (B) Sam stands up for himself and tells the bullies to leave him alone.
- (C) Sam walks home alone.
- (D) Sam yells at some other kids.

1. ☺ ☹

2. ☺ ☹

3. ☺ ☹

4. ☺ ☹

5. ☺ ☹

___ / 5
Total

NAME: _____ **DATE:** _____

Reread the text "No More Bullying."

Think about how Sam chose to confront his bullies.

Write about what you would do if you were being teased as you walked home.

_____

_____

_____

_____

_____

_____

_____

_____

_____

_____

NAME:_____ DATE:_____

DIRECTIONS Read the text and then answer the questions.

> People came to America long ago. They came before explorers landed. Native people lived across the land. The tribes lived a simple life. They took care of the land. It was their land, and they fought to keep it.

1. What is this text mostly about?

(A) explorers

(B) native people

(C) land

(D) a simple life

2. Where did native people live?

(A) on the plains

(B) on the coast

(C) where the explorers landed

(D) across America

3. What word has the same suffix as *lived*?

(A) hive

(B) love

(C) proved

(D) left

4. What is another word for *native*?

(A) a person who comes from a certain place

(B) a person who lives simply

(C) a person who lives in the woods

(D) a person who explores

NAME:_____ DATE:_____

DIRECTIONS Read the text and then answer the questions.

Buffalo are also known as *bison*. Buffalo are quite large. They can weigh around 2,000 pounds. Buffalo are fast, even though they are so large. They are good swimmers. They used to roam in huge numbers. Now they are found in smaller herds.

1. Which title best describes the main idea?

(A) Roaming Around

(B) Large and Fast

(C) Facts About Buffalo

(D) Small Herds

2. Which fact is **not** mentioned in the text?

(A) Buffalo were almost extinct because of hunting.

(B) Buffalo can weigh around 2,000 pounds.

(C) Buffalo are good swimmers.

(D) Buffalo are also called bison.

3. Which suffix **cannot** be added to the root word *swim*?

(A) –er

(B) –ly

(C) –s

(D) –able

4. What is another word for *roam*?

(A) wander

(B) eat

(C) herd

(D) hunt

NAME:_____ DATE:_____

DIRECTIONS Read the text and then answer the questions.

> Igloos are homes made from ice and snow. Inuit (IN-yoo-it) people live in them. Igloos are shaped like domes. Igloos are built in the arctic. There are not a lot of other materials to build with. Yet there is snow everywhere. Igloos are warm because the snow keeps warm air inside. Igloos can be big enough for one or two families.

1. ☺ ☺

2. ☺ ☺

3. ☺ ☺

4. ☺ ☺

1. What is the main topic?

(A) the arctic

(B) snow

(C) Inuit people

(D) igloos

2. What are igloos made of?

(A) ice

(B) snow

(C) ice and snow

(D) neither ice nor snow

3. Which word has the same suffix as the word *actually*?

(A) acting

(B) slowly

(C) punctual

(D) fly

4. Which is often in the shape of a *dome*?

(A) a tent

(B) a box lid

(C) a swimming pool

(D) a classroom

____ / 4

Total

NAME:_____ DATE:_____

American Indian Homes

American Indians live in tribes. These tribes lived in different parts of the country. Long ago, they built homes that helped them survive. The homes were made with special materials. Native people used what they had.

American Indians lived in many different types of homes. Some lived in grass houses. Tribes that lived on large, grassy plains used the grass to build homes. They worked well in warm climates. These structures were up to forty feet tall!

Adobe homes were a different type of home. They were called *pueblos* (PWEB-lohz). These homes were made of clay and straw. They often had more than one story! They worked well for tribes who stayed in one place for a long time. Pueblos helped keep people cool in hot weather.

Plank houses worked well in cold climates. Tribes that lived in plank houses built them out of wood. They worked well in cold places with forests nearby. The people found tall trees in the forests to make planks. Plank houses were also permanent houses.

Some tribes traveled a lot, so they built homes that could be easily moved. A *teepee* was one type of temporary home. A teepee looks like a tent. It is made of buffalo hide. Tribes that hunted buffalo built these homes.

teepees

All the tribes had to be smart builders. They used the materials they had nearby. They built structures to survive the climate. They were quite successful in creating their own types of communities.

NAME: _____ **DATE:** _____

DIRECTIONS Read "American Indian Homes" and then answer the questions.

1. Which example shows a connection to the text?

(A) I have grass in my backyard.

(B) Our house is built strong for hurricanes.

(C) I make pottery with clay.

(D) I have seen buffalo at the zoo.

2. What type of house works well in a cold climate?

(A) a plank house

(B) a blank house

(C) a pink house

(D) a plunk house

3. Based on context clues, what is a buffalo *hide*?

(A) the skin

(B) the teeth

(C) the feet

(D) the head

4. What do adobe and grass houses have in common?

(A) They are both easy to move.

(B) They are both made of grass.

(C) They both work well in warmer climates.

(D) They both use wood.

5. Which is the best summary of the text?

(A) Plank houses were made from wood.

(B) Tribes built homes that were easily moveable.

(C) Tribes built houses that met their needs.

(D) American Indians lived in teepees.

1. ☺ ☺

2. ☺ ☺

3. ☺ ☺

4. ☺ ☺

5. ☺ ☺

____ / 5
Total

NAME:_____ **DATE:**_____

 Reread the text "American Indian Homes."

 Think about how these homes are similar and different.

 Write about two similarities and two differences you notice about the homes.

_____

_____

_____

_____

_____

_____

_____

_____

_____

_____

_____

_____

NAME:_____ **DATE:**_____

DIRECTIONS Read the text and then answer the questions.

Some kids played a game called Telephone. Casey and John got four kids together, and they all sat in a circle. Casey came up with a funny sentence. She whispered it to the friend on her left. That friend whispered it to the next friend. The story traveled around the circle. When it got to John, he said the sentence aloud. The kids all laughed! The sentence was not the same at all!

1. ☺ ☺

2. ☺ ☺

3. ☺ ☺

4. ☺ ☺

____ / 4

Total

1. What makes the game of Telephone so fun and silly?

(A) It is hard to hear someone whispering.

(B) The message at the end does not match the message at the beginning.

(C) Sitting in a circle is silly.

(D) John keeps telling jokes.

2. Which title best fits the text?

(A) Calling Your Friends

(B) The Game of Telephone

(C) Funny Statements

(D) Whispered Words

3. How many syllables are in the word *telephone*?

(A) one syllable

(B) two syllables

(C) three syllables

(D) four syllables

4. What does it mean that the story *traveled around the circle*?

(A) It was a story about a vacation trip.

(B) The story went on and on.

(C) The story had no ending.

(D) The story was told from one kid to the next, around the circle.

NAME:_____ DATE:_____

DIRECTIONS Read the text and then answer the questions.

1. ☺ ☹

2. ☺ ☹

3. ☺ ☹

4. ☺ ☹

_____ / 4
Total

My grandpa always told stories. It was hard to know what was true. I don't know if he really did walk eight miles to school in the snow. I also wonder if he saw a real bear that day in the woods, but it doesn't really matter. What matters is that he told me the tales. I loved my grandpa's company.

1. Who is the narrator?

(A) a bear

(B) a grandson

(C) a grandma

(D) a grandpa

2. Which title best fits the text?

(A) Jokes from My Family

(B) Special Times with My Grandpa

(C) Tall Tales

(D) A Walk in the Snow

3. Which word **cannot** be added to the word *snow* to make a compound word?

(A) flake

(B) suit

(C) man

(D) hill

4. What does the word *company* mean in the last sentence?

(A) a business

(B) work

(C) being together

(D) group

NAME:_____ DATE:_____

DIRECTIONS Read the text and then answer the questions.

We talked about George Washington in school today. He was the first president. There are many stories about him. One is that he could not tell a lie. As a child, he got caught cutting down a cherry tree. The tree was a special one. His father was furious. George told the truth. His father was happy that he told the truth. That story has been told for over 200 years! I could not believe that!

1. What does the narrator think is unusual about the George Washington story?

Ⓐ Cutting down a cherry tree was a big deal.

Ⓑ The president was so honest.

Ⓒ His dad was mad.

Ⓓ It has been told for over 200 years.

2. Who does *we* refer to in the first sentence?

Ⓐ a family

Ⓑ an author

Ⓒ a class of students

Ⓓ George Washington

3. Which word has the same root word *talked*?

Ⓐ stalker

Ⓑ walked

Ⓒ talking

Ⓓ taller

4. What does *furious* mean?

Ⓐ appalled

Ⓑ curious

Ⓒ interested

Ⓓ very angry

NAME:_____ DATE:_____

Johnny Appleseed

Johnny Appleseed lived long ago. He was born in 1774. His real name was John Chapman. He was famous for planting apple trees.

Some stories claim that he just spread seeds around. But Johnny knew a lot about trees. He knew where they should grow. He set up *nurseries*. These are places for trees to grow. The trees were sold to people. Then people planted the trees on their land.

Johnny wanted apple trees to grow over large areas of land. He wanted to protect things in nature.

This story has been passed down over the years. Some facts are true. Some facts have been exaggerated. It is a folktale that many people know.

One reason Johnny Appleseed is famous is because he was a warm and kind man. He treated others very nicely. He lived a simple life. He cared deeply about animals and looked after things in nature. He is a hero. He is admired for his good nature and his good deeds.

 #50923—*180 Days of Reading for Second Grade*

NAME:_____ **DATE:**_____

DIRECTIONS Read "Johnny Appleseed" and then answer the questions.

1. Who might make a connection to the text?

(A) a little girl who does not like to eat apples

(B) a teacher who is warm and kind to children

(C) a young boy who cleans up local beaches

(D) a man who plants seeds in his garden

2. What kind of story is "Johnny Appleseed"?

(A) a foketale

(B) a folktale

(C) a fulltale

(D) a folktall

3. What is a *hero*?

(A) a strong person

(B) a person who lives a simple life

(C) a person who is admired by others

(D) a person who lived long ago

4. Where did Johnny Appleseed get his nickname?

(A) He planted apple trees and protected large areas of nature.

(B) He bought and sold apples.

(C) He baked apple pies.

(D) He was good to animals and people.

5. Which gives the best summary?

(A) Johnny Appleseed is a famous farmer.

(B) Johnny Appleseed's life story is a folktale that many people know.

(C) Johnny Appleseed invented the apple.

(D) Johnny Appleseed knew a lot about trees.

1. ☺ ☺

2. ☺ ☺

3. ☺ ☺

4. ☺ ☺

5. ☺ ☺

___ / 5
Total

SCORE

___ / 4

NAME:_____ **DATE:**_____

 Reread the text "Johnny Appleseed."

 Think about the reasons why Johnny Appleseed is a hero.

Write about a hero in your own life. Why do you admire this person?

_____

_____

_____

_____

_____

_____

_____

_____

_____

_____

_____

NAME: _____ **DATE:** _____

DIRECTIONS Read the text and then answer the questions.

Sunscreen is important. It protects skin from sunburns. Yet, not all sun exposure is bad. Getting some sun can be good for you. Our bodies make vitamin D. They only do this while getting sun. Vitamin D is important for our health, too. A few minutes of sunshine each day is all you need.

1. ☺ ☹

2. ☺ ☹

3. ☺ ☹

4. ☺ ☹

___ / 4
Total

1. What is the important point about being in the sun?

(A) People should avoid the sun.

(B) Vitamin D comes from sunscreen.

(C) Getting some sun is important for our bodies to make vitamin D.

(D) Sunscreen should be worn every day.

2. When do our bodies make vitamin D?

(A) when we exercise

(B) when we are in the sun

(C) when we use sunscreen

(D) in the morning

3. Which word is **not** a compound word?

(A) sunshine

(B) sunburn

(C) sunscreen

(D) vitamin

4. What is the meaning of the word *exposure* in this text?

(A) body

(B) contact

(C) sun

(D) warmth

NAME:_____ DATE:_____

SCORE

1. ☺ ☺

2. ☺ ☺

3. ☺ ☺

4. ☺ ☺

____ / 4
Total

DIRECTIONS Read the text and then answer the questions.

Bobcats can live almost anywhere. Many of them are found in the desert. A bobcat looks a lot like a large house cat. But bobcats are bigger. They also have a fierce growl. Some people say that a bobcat sounds like a mountain lion. Bobcats like to prey on rabbits, mice, and rats. They are good hunters.

1. What is the main topic?

- Ⓐ bobcats
- Ⓑ rabbits
- Ⓒ hunters
- Ⓓ mountain lions

2. What does a bobcat look like?

- Ⓐ a house cat
- Ⓑ a mountain lion
- Ⓒ a rabbit
- Ⓓ a mouse

3. What is the root word in *hunters*?

- Ⓐ hunter
- Ⓑ ters
- Ⓒ unt
- Ⓓ hunt

4. Which of these animals does not have a *fierce growl*?

- Ⓐ leopard
- Ⓑ tiger
- Ⓒ lion
- Ⓓ elephant

#50923—180 Days of Reading for Second Grade

NAME: _____ **DATE:** _____

DIRECTIONS Read the text and then answer the questions.

Cactus plants are very common in the desert. One type of cactus that grows in the desert is called a *prickly pear*. It can grow in sandy ground. This plant can survive hot and dry days. It can also live through freezing mornings. That is quite a range of temperatures! A prickly pear grows up to seven feet tall.

1. ☺ ☹

2. ☺ ☹

3. ☺ ☹

4. ☺ ☹

1. What is this text mostly about?

(A) desert animals

(B) temperatures

(C) prickly pear cactus

(D) sand

2. What is most unusual about a prickly pear?

(A) It is a cactus.

(B) It can survive in both high and low temperatures.

(C) It is in the desert.

(D) It likes the sun.

3. Which word has the same root word as *grows*?

(A) rows

(B) owes

(C) growing

(D) wing

4. What does *common* mean in the first sentence?

(A) friendly

(B) rare

(C) familiar

(D) shared

___ / 4
Total

NAME: _____ DATE: _____

Comparing Biomes

The desert is a special place. It is very dry. There is little rain there. Desert plants and animals can live without a lot of water. The cactus lives there. It stores water in its trunk. This helps it survive in the heat.

desert biome

The desert is one type of biome. A *biome* is an area with certain plants and animals. The entire area has the same climate. These things make the area unique.

The tundra is another kind of biome. The tundra is very cold. Not many plants or trees can survive there. Some bushes and shrubs live there. Animals, such as foxes and bears, can live there, too. They have to endure cold and wind.

A tropical rainforest is also a biome. It gets a lot of rain. It is also a very warm region. Large rainforests have animal and plant life. They can survive in damp and warm spaces. Various monkey species live in this biome.

Each biome is unique. People have to protect all biomes. Many living things depend on us. They want a healthy habitat.

NAME: _____ **DATE:** _____

DIRECTIONS Read "Comparing Biomes" and then answer the questions.

1. Who might make a connection to the text?

Ⓐ a person who has visited a desert

Ⓑ an author who is writing about weather

Ⓒ a child who likes to draw monkeys

Ⓓ a weatherman who studies hurricanes

2. Which word describes an animal that lives in the tundra?

Ⓐ a fax

Ⓑ a sox

Ⓒ a fox

Ⓓ a fix

3. What does the word *endure* mean?

Ⓐ enjoy

Ⓑ tolerate

Ⓒ exit

Ⓓ watch

4. Which is true for all biomes?

Ⓐ All biomes are wet.

Ⓑ All biomes are cold.

Ⓒ All biomes are unique.

Ⓓ All biomes are full of people.

5. According to the author, what do people need to do for biomes?

Ⓐ Protect them so that they are healthy habitats.

Ⓑ Measure the rainfall in rainforests.

Ⓒ Stay away from hot and dry deserts.

Ⓓ Locate animals in each biome.

1. ☺ ☺

2. ☺ ☺

3. ☺ ☺

4. ☺ ☺

5. ☺ ☺

___ / 5
Total

NAME: _____ **DATE:** _____

 Reread the text "Comparing Biomes."

 Think about how biomes are similar and different.

 Write about how the desert, tundra, and tropical rainforest differ.

_____

_____

_____

_____

_____

_____

_____

_____

_____

_____

_____

_____

NAME:_____ **DATE:**_____

DIRECTIONS Read the text and then answer the questions.

Our class took a survey today. We each chose our favorite pizza topping. We worked together to tally the results. I was not surprised. Pepperoni won, with fifteen votes. Cheese came in second place. It got six votes. Veggie and sausage tied for last. They each got three votes. Our class sure loves pepperoni pizza!

1.☺☺

2.☺☺

3.☺☺

4.☺☺

1. What is the correct order of the survey results?

Ⓐ cheese, pepperoni, veggie and sausage

Ⓑ pepperoni, cheese, veggie and sausage

Ⓒ cheese, veggie and sausage, pepperoni

Ⓓ veggie and sausage, cheese, pepperoni

2. What is the text mostly about?

Ⓐ a class survey and its results

Ⓑ pizza delivery

Ⓒ veggie pizza

Ⓓ voting

3. Which suffix can be added to *work* to make a new word?

Ⓐ –ly

Ⓑ –er

Ⓒ –tion

Ⓓ –or

4. Which statement describes a *survey*?

Ⓐ a graph

Ⓑ answers to a poll about an opinion or preference

Ⓒ an official investigation

Ⓓ an election

____/4
Total

NAME:_____ DATE:_____

SCORE

1. ☺ ☺

2. ☺ ☺

3. ☺ ☺

4. ☺ ☺

____ / 4
Total

DIRECTIONS Read the text and then answer the questions.

Liam went to the polling place with his dad. This was a big day. Everyone was voting for a new president. Liam's dad thought he should show his son how it all works. Liam got to see the ballot, and he watched his dad make choices. When he finished, Liam's dad put the ballot in a box. Liam went home with a sticker that said, "I Voted."

1. Where does the text take place?

- (A) election day
- (B) a ballot box
- (C) a polling place
- (D) a school

2. What important lessons does Liam learn from this experience?

- (A) He learns about new stickers.
- (B) He learns who the best president will be.
- (C) He learns about how and where to vote.
- (D) He learns about where his dad works.

3. Which word from the text can have the *–ing* suffix added to make a new word?

- (A) big
- (B) went
- (C) make
- (D) day

4. What does *polling place* mean?

- (A) a place for a dad to play with his son
- (B) a place that gives out stickers
- (C) a place for the president to visit
- (D) a place where election voting takes place

NAME:_____ DATE:_____

DIRECTIONS Read the text and then answer the questions.

Students are proud of their school, so school issues are important to them. They want to be heard by grown-ups. They have a lot of opinions about how to make things better. Ask a young student about school. You will hear some fresh ideas!

1. 😊 😐

2. 😊 😐

3. 😊 😐

1. What is important to students?

(A) grown-ups

(B) school issues

(C) opinions

(D) ideas

2. What does the text say about students?

(A) Students don't like to talk about school.

(B) Students only care about their own issues.

(C) Students' opinions should be heard because they want to make their school a great place.

(D) Students' opinions are not as important as what the teachers say.

3. Which word from the text can have the *–er* suffix added to make a new word?

(A) grown

(B) proud

(C) school

(D) better

4. Which of the following would **not** be a student *opinion* about a school?

(A) The school should recycle the lunch trays.

(B) The school should have a toy drive for the holidays.

(C) The school was built in 1965.

(D) The school needs a safer playground.

4. 😊 😐

___/ 4

Total

NAME: _____ DATE: _____

Election Day

The students were voting at lunch. Today was election day. The school was picking a student council. Each class sends one person to the council. The council meets with teachers. It also talks to the principal. It gives the students a voice. They share opinions about the school. They talk about cafeteria food. They discuss lunch recess rules. They even have ideas they want to get going.

Students signed up for the council. Sometimes only one student in a class wants the job. That makes it easy to choose! In other classes, two or three students have to battle it out. They need the highest number of votes to win.

Students practice real ways to run for office. They give speeches. They talk about issues. They make promises. All of these things happen in a real election, too.

Finally, it's time to vote. Students go into a polling place. They choose a name. They put their ballot in the box. The principal counts the votes. The school council is formed!

Now the council can get to the hard work. They can come together to make the school a great place to be!

NAME:_____ DATE:_____

DIRECTIONS Read "Election Day" and then answer the questions.

1. Who might make a connection to the text?

(A) a teacher who is planning a lesson

(B) a store owner who is angry at customers

(C) a student who wants to clean up trash at school

(D) a babysitter who is in charge of several kids

2. What could be a different title for this text?

(A) Polling Place

(B) Voting for Student Council

(C) Recess Rules

(D) Ballots

3. What does *battle it out* mean?

(A) disagree

(B) compete

(C) go to war

(D) play

4. What is the text about?

(A) talking to the principal

(B) discussing school issues

(C) voting for a student council

(D) writing a speech

5. Which best summarizes the text?

(A) Talking to the principal about problems is hard.

(B) A student council election is similar to a real election.

(C) Polling places are fun to visit.

(D) A school that needs a lot done requires smart people to help.

1.☺☹

2.☺☹

3.☺☹

4.☺☹

5.☺☹

___/5
Total

NAME: _____ **DATE:** _____

 Reread the text "Election Day."

 Think about what a student council can do for your school.

 Write about the issues you would want to talk about with other council members if you were a student council member.

_____

_____

_____

_____

_____

_____

_____

_____

_____

_____

_____

NAME:_____ **DATE:**_____

DIRECTIONS Read the text and then answer the questions.

> Many people enjoy baseball. It is a popular sport. A lot of people follow the major league. There are a lot of teams. The Chicago Cubs is one team. They have played since 1876. They are the oldest team to stay in the same city.

1. 🙂 😐

2. 🙂 😐

3. 🙂 😐

4. 🙂 😐

____ / 4
Total

1. What is special about the Chicago Cubs?

Ⓐ They are part of the major league.

Ⓑ People enjoy watching them.

Ⓒ They are the oldest team to stay in the same city.

Ⓓ They win a lot of games.

2. When were the Chicago Cubs formed?

Ⓐ 1877

Ⓑ 1786

Ⓒ 1867

Ⓓ 1876

3. What is the root word in *oldest*?

Ⓐ *old*

Ⓑ *est*

Ⓒ *dest*

Ⓓ *st*

4. Using context clues, what does *league* mean?

Ⓐ It is a group of sports teams that play against each other.

Ⓑ It is a team that has played for a long time.

Ⓒ It is a team in Chicago.

Ⓓ It is a soccer group.

NAME: _____ **DATE:** _____

SCORE

1. ☺ ☻

2. ☺ ☻

3. ☺ ☻

4. ☺ ☻

____ / 4

Total

DIRECTIONS Read the text and then answer the questions.

People are not always treated the same. This unequal treatment is called *discrimination*. In the past, men had more rights than women. Women could not vote, own a house, or have a job. They were second-class citizens. This has all changed, but it has taken many years for change to come. Laws have been passed to make sure it stays this way. Today, women in most places have the same rights as men.

1. What is the main idea?

Ⓐ Women can now vote.

Ⓑ Discrimination against women has changed.

Ⓒ Women became second-class citizens.

Ⓓ Women and men do not have the same rights.

2. Why is discrimination no longer allowed?

Ⓐ It happened to men.

Ⓑ It is hard to find a job for everyone.

Ⓒ It is against the law now.

Ⓓ Women today still can't do what men can.

3. What is the suffix in the word *changed*?

Ⓐ *–ed*

Ⓑ *–ged*

Ⓒ *change*

Ⓓ *ch–*

4. Which words mean similar things?

Ⓐ *treated* and *changed*

Ⓑ *women* and *men*

Ⓒ *citizens* and *people*

Ⓓ *discrimination* and *laws*

NAME:_____ **DATE:**_____

DIRECTIONS Read the text and then answer the questions.

Rosa Parks stood up for herself. Rosa Parks was African American. She had to give up her seat to a white person. This was the law. One day in 1955, she refused to follow that law. She was riding on the bus. She would not give up her seat. She was arrested. Her actions changed the world. The civil rights movement was born.

1. 🙂 😐

2. 🙂 😐

3. 🙂 😐

4. 🙂 😐

____/ 4

Total

1. What is this text mostly about?

(A) a bus seat

(B) the civil rights movement

(C) old laws

(D) Rosa Parks

3. How would the word *movement* be divided into syllables?

(A) mov-ement

(B) mo-vement

(C) move-ment

(D) movem-ent

2. Which is **not** true?

(A) Rosa Parks refused to give up her seat on a bus.

(B) Rosa Parks was born in 1955.

(C) Rosa Parks was a brave woman.

(D) Rosa Parks was arrested.

4. Which means *stood up for herself*?

(A) was uncertain

(B) stayed healthy

(C) had courage

(D) was shocking

NAME:_____ DATE:_____

An Inspirational Man

Jackie Robinson was a baseball player. He was famous. He was a good man. He was born in 1919. He was African American. His life was difficult. People were not always nice to his family. It was a hard time.

Jackie was a good athlete. He loved many sports. He went to college. Jackie joined the army. Then he made a choice. He began to play baseball.

This was in 1944. Baseball teams were separate. White players had their own leagues. Jackie was chosen for a team. It was a team of only white players. It was a hard time for him. Some people wanted Jackie to go away. They wanted him on another team. Some of his teammates agreed. Other teams did not want to play against him.

Jackie Robinson

But not all people felt like this. Some stood up for Jackie. His manager was loyal to him. This helped others treat Jackie better. People began to change their minds.

Jackie showed that he could play ball. He was an amazing athlete. He changed people's minds. That was a victory!

NAME:_____ DATE:_____

DIRECTIONS Read "An Inspirational Man" and then answer the questions.

1. Which shows a connection to the text?

(A) I need to learn to play baseball.

(B) I am angry when people do not include me.

(C) I work through hard times and don't give up.

(D) When life is tough, it's time to take a break.

2. How does the author describe Jackie's life?

(A) It was easy.

(B) It was scary.

(C) It was nice.

(D) It was difficult.

3. What does *loyal* mean?

(A) upset with someone

(B) expressing support and dedication for someone

(C) playing nicely with someone

(D) ignoring someone

4. Jackie had a difficult life because

(A) he had the flu.

(B) he was African American.

(C) he was bad at baseball.

(D) he was not very famous.

5. Which best summarizes Jackie Robinson's experience?

(A) Jackie was an amazing baseball player who took advantage of a lucky opportunity.

(B) Jackie was an amazing baseball player who stood out from the crowd.

(C) Jackie was an amazing baseball player who was focused on the game.

(D) Jackie was an amazing baseball player who stood up for himself and taught people to be open-minded.

1. ☺ ☺

2. ☺ ☺

3. ☺ ☺

4. ☺ ☺

5. ☺ ☺

___ / 5

Total

NAME: _____ **DATE:** _____

 Reread the text "An Inspirational Man."

 Think about what Jackie Robinson's life experiences must have felt like to him.

Write about the qualities that Jackie Robinson showed to others. How did these qualities help him?

_____

_____

_____

_____

_____

_____

_____

_____

_____

_____

_____

_____

_____

NAME:_____ **DATE:**_____

DIRECTIONS Read the text and then answer the questions.

> The lobby is very busy. Lines are endless. People are cranky. Checking in luggage takes a long time. Going through the security gate is a lot of work, too. Finally, it is time to get on board. The plane is almost ready to take off!

1. ☺ ☹

2. ☺ ☹

1. What is the setting?

(A) a museum

(B) an airport

(C) a train station

(D) a luggage store

3. Which word has a suffix that means *without*?

(A) lobby

(B) luggage

(C) endless

(D) security

3. ☺ ☹

4. ☺ ☹

___ / 4
Total

2. What is the main idea?

(A) Planning your vacation ahead of time is always a good idea.

(B) Sometimes traveling is difficult.

(C) Don't overpack a suitcase.

(D) All airports are crowded.

4. Which word means the opposite of *endless* as it is used in this text?

(A) quick

(B) straight

(C) growing

(D) extreme

NAME:_____ DATE:_____

SCORE

1. ☺ ☹

2. ☺ ☹

3. ☺ ☹

4. ☺ ☹

____ / 4

Total

DIRECTIONS Read the text and then answer the questions.

"What is there to do out here?" Jackson's cousin asked him.

"There is so much to do!" Jackson replied. "We don't even have enough time to see everything here." Jackson lived on a farm. His home was miles away from any city. He had no neighbors. Yet Jackson was never bored. He had animals to play with and space to explore. He could not imagine life in the city with his cousin.

1. What does the boys' conversation tell you?

(A) They are the same age.

(B) They might live in different places.

(C) They are both afraid of horses.

(D) They have not seen each other in a while.

2. What is life like on a farm?

(A) It can be very exciting.

(B) Farms are always big.

(C) All kids should like to explore outside.

(D) Being in the city means you are much busier.

3. What is a homophone of *hear*?

(A) here

(B) heer

(C) heir

(D) hare

4. What does it mean that Jackson has *space to explore*?

(A) He can see stars clearly out in the country.

(B) He doesn't have a brother or sister, so he has room to move around.

(C) His barn is two stories.

(D) His farmland has a lot of places to check out.

NAME:_____ DATE:_____

DIRECTIONS Read the text and then answer the questions.

1. ☺ ☺

   The boat trip was quiet. I was with my family. We were thinking of our ancestors. They had come this way before. They had seen the Statue of Liberty. They came to America many years ago. Life was different then. They wanted a better place to live. We all felt grateful they had come here.

2. ☺ ☺

3. ☺ ☺

1. What is the setting?

3. Which word from the text has a root word?

4. ☺ ☺

(A) on a boat

(B) on an airplane

(C) on an island

(D) on a statue

(A) wanted

(B) grateful

(C) liberty

(D) better

____/ 4
Total

2. Why is this trip special to this family?

(A) because trips in America are always fun

(B) because they enjoy quiet trips

(C) because the Statue of Liberty is a special monument

(D) because their ancestors had traveled the same route

4. Which word is the past tense of *thinking*?

(A) thoughts

(B) thunk

(C) thought

(D) thank

NAME:_____ DATE:_____

The Trip of a Lifetime

Nick was so excited. It was three days until his big trip. He was going to New York City. Nick had never been there. This was his first train trip. His parents had been saving money all year long. They wanted to take the whole family. They wanted to visit a new and exciting place.

Nick wanted to keep a trip journal. A journal would help him remember what he did on this trip. He wanted to be able to look back and reminisce about good times in New York.

Nick talked to his mother. He knew he could write descriptions in his journal. But what about things he saw that were really interesting? He wanted to take pictures. Nick's family had a camera. But it was broken. He decided to borrow a camera from his friend, Anthony. He promised to take good care of it. He would use the camera to take pictures on the trip. After he came home, he would make a scrapbook of the journey.

The night before the trip, Nick packed the camera, pen, and journal. He could barely sleep. He wished that morning would come so he could go to the train station.

In the morning, Nick and his family boarded the train. They were on their way to New York. Nick began to write in his journal. He started taking a lot of pictures. He was going to have the trip of a lifetime.

NAME:_____ DATE:_____

DIRECTIONS Read "The Trip of a Lifetime" and then answer the questions.

1. Why is it a good idea to create a journal on a vacation?

(A) It is how you will know the history of a place you visit.

(B) It is a way to remember a special time.

(C) It helps you know how to get around in a new town.

(D) It is a way to keep secrets from everyone.

2. How does Nick travel to New York?

(A) on a train

(B) on a tram

(C) in a truck

(D) on a trail

3. Using context clues, what is the meaning of the word *reminisce*?

(A) remember

(B) regret

(C) forget

(D) refute

4. How do you know that Nick is excited?

(A) He cannot eat.

(B) He goes on a train.

(C) He cannot sleep.

(D) He saves his money.

5. Which of the following does Nick **not** bring with him to New York?

(A) a camera

(B) a journal

(C) a pen

(D) a scrapbook

1. ☺ ☺

2. ☺ ☺

3. ☺ ☺

4. ☺ ☺

5. ☺ ☺

___ / 5
Total

NAME: _____ **DATE:** _____

 Reread the text "The Trip of a Lifetime."

 Think about how this trip to New York was important to Nick.

Write about a trip you took that you remember. What made your trip special?

_____

_____

_____

_____

_____

_____

_____

_____

_____

_____

_____

NAME:_____ DATE:_____

DIRECTIONS Read the text and then answer the questions.

> A lot of people live in big cities. Many of them do not own cars. Driving and parking can be a hassle. So they get around in other ways. A *subway* is one way to get around. It is an underground train. It takes people to different stops. Residents can ride the subway day and night.

1. ☺ ☻

2. ☺ ☻

3. ☺ ☻

4. ☺ ☻

___ / 4
Total

1. What is the main idea?

(A) Cities are usually big.

(B) Driving a car is difficult in the city.

(C) A subway is one way that people get around cities.

(D) Subways are always open.

2. What is one reason that people do **not** own cars in the city?

(A) Parking is difficult.

(B) There are too many places to stop.

(C) There are too many people.

(D) It costs too much.

3. Which is the compound word in the text?

(A) around

(B) underground

(C) driving

(D) hassle

4. Using context clues, what does *hassle* mean?

(A) big

(B) underground

(C) difficult

(D) parking

NAME:_____ DATE:_____

SCORE

1. ☺ ☹

2. ☺ ☹

3. ☺ ☹

4. ☺ ☹

____ / 4
Total

DIRECTIONS Read the text and then answer the questions.

Cities make sure people are safe. They create a police force. They have fire departments. They help plan new buildings and roads. The city even helps to run the library and keep parks clean. A city government does a lot for the people who live there.

1. Which title might best describe a city government?

- (A) Letting People Down
- (B) Libraries and Parks
- (C) Doing So Much for So Many
- (D) Building Safe Schools

2. What does a city **not** do for its residents?

- (A) run the library
- (B) create a police force
- (C) clean houses
- (D) keep parks clean

3. Which word has the same root word as *government*?

- (A) department
- (B) governor
- (C) testament
- (D) tavern

4. Which word means *safe*?

- (A) warm
- (B) fed
- (C) secure
- (D) alive

NAME:_____ DATE:_____

DIRECTIONS Read the text and then answer the questions.

Tractors help with farmwork. Farmers rely on them, since they make farmwork easier. A tractor can pull along a plow. This helps to turn over the soil to plant crops in a field. A farmer can get an entire field ready for planting in just a few hours!

1. ☺ ☺

2. ☺ ☺

3. ☺ ☺

1. Which word best describes the main idea about tractors?

(A) difficult

(B) planting

(C) heavy

(D) helpful

2. What does a plow do?

(A) It pulls a tractor.

(B) It turns over the soil for planting crops.

(C) It harvests crops.

(D) It waters crops.

3. How many syllables are in the word *tractor*?

(A) one syllable

(B) two syllables

(C) three syllables

(D) four syllables

4. ☺ ☺

_____/4
Total

4. Which word means *soil*?

(A) crop

(B) dirt

(C) plant

(D) rock

NAME: _____ DATE: _____

City and Country Living

Life in the city is not like country living. *Urban* areas have more people. People live closer together in cities. There are more buildings. Big cities have more cars and roads. Some say that life moves faster in the city. There is always a lot going on. People are out at all times. It can be loud.

People in *rural* areas have space to move. They live close to nature. They may even grow plants or raise animals for a living. Life is quiet there. They do not hear the sounds of the city.

a rural area

Suburbs are found in between the city and the country. These smaller towns border big cities. Some say that life in the suburbs is better than in the city. Suburbs are smaller and quieter. It may be easier for people to get around. Many families live there. There are parks for kids. Adults can commute to the city for work.

Cities, suburbs, and rural areas can be close together. A large city may be surrounded by suburbs. Just beyond the suburbs are quieter, rural areas. It may take a few hours to get there.

Sometimes city dwellers like to visit the country. Country folks may like to spend time in the city, too. Most people are happy to go back home, wherever that may be.

NAME:_____ DATE:_____

DIRECTIONS Read "City and Country Living" and then answer the questions.

1. What can all readers learn from this text?

Ⓐ Life in other places can be good, too.

Ⓑ Life in the country is boring.

Ⓒ Cities are loud and dirty.

Ⓓ Suburbs are only for families.

2. What do some people do to get to work in a nearby city?

Ⓐ commit

Ⓑ compute

Ⓒ commute

Ⓓ committee

3. Who are *city dwellers*?

Ⓐ people who like cities

Ⓑ people who live in cities

Ⓒ people who hate cities

Ⓓ people who commute to cities

4. Does the author claim that life is better in the city, the country, or the suburbs?

Ⓐ the city

Ⓑ the country

Ⓒ the suburbs

Ⓓ Each place has good things to offer.

5. Which statement does the author make?

Ⓐ Most people wish they lived in the country.

Ⓑ Most people are happy that they live where they do.

Ⓒ People who live in the city have no interest in visiting the country.

Ⓓ Suburbs are for people who enjoy driving.

1. ☺ ☹

2. ☺ ☹

3. ☺ ☹

4. ☺ ☹

5. ☺ ☹

___ / 5
Total

NAME: _____ **DATE:** _____

 Reread the text "City and Country Living."

 Think about how living in the country and the city are different.

 Write about the perfect place to live. What makes this place so great?

_____

_____

_____

_____

_____

_____

_____

_____

_____

_____

_____

_____

ANSWER KEY

Week 1

Day 1
1. B
2. D
3. D
4. C

Day 2
1. D
2. C
3. A
4. C

Day 3
1. C
2. A
3. B
4. C

Day 4
1. A
2. D
3. A
4. B
5. D

Day 5
Responses will vary.

Week 2

Day 1
1. D
2. C
3. C
4. A

Day 2
1. B
2. D
3. B
4. C

Day 3
1. B
2. C
3. B
4. C

Day 4
1. C
2. B
3. B
4. C
5. A

Day 5
Responses will vary.

Week 3

Day 1
1. B
2. B
3. B
4. A

Day 2
1. A
2. C
3. A
4. D

Day 3
1. D
2. C
3. B
4. B

Day 4
1. B
2. A
3. A
4. B
5. D

Day 5
Responses will vary.

Week 4

Day 1
1. A
2. D
3. B
4. C

Day 2
1. C
2. D
3. B
4. A

Day 3
1. B
2. C
3. B
4. C

Day 4
1. B
2. A
3. C
4. C
5. C

Day 5
Responses will vary.

Week 5

Day 1
1. C
2. B
3. C
4. D

Day 2
1. A
2. C
3. A
4. B

Day 3
1. B
2. A
3. D
4. B

Day 4
1. C
2. D
3. C
4. D
5. A

Day 5
Responses will vary.

Week 6

Day 1
1. B
2. D
3. B
4. D

Day 2
1. C
2. B
3. B
4. B

Day 3
1. B
2. C
3. B
4. C

Day 4
1. A
2. D
3. A
4. B
5. B

Day 5
Responses will vary.

Week 7

Day 1
1. B
2. A
3. B
4. C

Day 2
1. B
2. A
3. A
4. C

Day 3
1. B
2. C
3. B
4. A

ANSWER KEY *(cont.)*

Week 7 *(cont.)*

Day 4
1. C
2. C
3. D
4. B
5. D

Day 5
Responses will vary.

Week 8

Day 1
1. A
2. C
3. B
4. D

Day 2
1. B
2. B
3. C
4. A

Day 3
1. B
2. D
3. C
4. C

Day 4
1. C
2. B
3. A
4. D
5. C

Day 5
Responses will vary.

Week 9

Day 1
1. C
2. C
3. D
4. B

Day 2
1. B
2. A
3. B
4. D

Day 3
1. A
2. C
3. B
4. A

Day 4
1. B
2. C
3. B
4. D
5. A

Day 5
Responses will vary.

Week 10

Day 1
1. C
2. B
3. A
4. B

Day 2
1. B
2. B
3. C
4. D

Day 3
1. B
2. D
3. B
4. A

Day 4
1. B
2. A
3. D
4. D
5. C

Day 5
Responses will vary.

Week 11

Day 1
1. B
2. D
3. A
4. C

Day 2
1. A
2. C
3. B
4. B

Day 3
1. C
2. C
3. C
4. B

Day 4
1. D
2. C
3. B
4. D
5. B

Day 5
Responses will vary.

Week 12

Day 1
1. C
2. D
3. A
4. D

Day 2
1. C
2. B
3. B
4. C

Day 3
1. B
2. B
3. A
4. C

ANSWER KEY *(cont.)*

Week 12 *(cont.)*

Day 4
1. C
2. B
3. D
4. D
5. C

Day 5
Responses will vary.

Week 13

Day 1
1. C
2. D
3. C
4. D

Day 2
1. B
2. B
3. D
4. D

Day 3
1. A
2. B
3. B
4. C

Day 4
1. A
2. C
3. B
4. B
5. D

Day 5
Responses will vary.

Week 14

Day 1
1. C
2. D
3. D
4. A

Day 2
1. B
2. C
3. B
4. C

Day 3
1. B
2. C
3. A
4. B

Day 4
1. C
2. B
3. C
4. C
5. D

Day 5
Responses will vary.

Week 15

Day 1
1. A
2. B
3. D
4. A

Day 2
1. C
2. B
3. D
4. A

Day 3
1. A
2. D
3. D
4. B

Day 4
1. D
2. A
3. C
4. C
5. B

Day 5
Responses will vary.

Week 16

Day 1
1. C
2. C
3. B
4. C

Day 2
1. A
2. B
3. D
4. A

Day 3
1. D
2. C
3. C
4. B

Day 4
1. C
2. D
3. D
4. C
5. C

Day 5
Responses will vary.

Week 17

Day 1
1. C
2. A
3. A
4. B

Day 2
1. B
2. B
3. B
4. B

Day 3
1. A
2. C
3. B
4. D

ANSWER KEY (cont.)

Week 17 (cont.)

Day 4
1. C
2. A
3. C
4. B
5. C

Day 5
Responses will vary.

Week 18

Day 1
1. C
2. A
3. B
4. B

Day 2
1. B
2. A
3. C
4. D

Day 3
1. D
2. C
3. B
4. D

Day 4
1. B
2. B
3. B
4. D
5. A

Day 5
Responses will vary.

Week 19

Day 1
1. C
2. B
3. A
4. D

Day 2
1. B
2. D
3. A
4. C

Day 3
1. B
2. B
3. C
4. A

Day 4
1. A
2. B
3. B
4. B
5. D

Day 5
Responses will vary.

Week 20

Day 1
1. C
2. A
3. C
4. B

Day 2
1. D
2. B
3. B
4. C

Day 3
1. A
2. C
3. D
4. B

Day 4
1. D
2. D
3. B
4. A
5. C

Day 5
Responses will vary.

Week 21

Day 1
1. B
2. C
3. B
4. C

Day 2
1. A
2. D
3. B
4. B

Day 3
1. A
2. C
3. B
4. D

Day 4
1. D
2. A
3. C
4. D
5. A

Day 5
Responses will vary.

Week 22

Day 1
1. B
2. A
3. D
4. B

Day 2
1. B
2. B
3. C
4. D

Day 3
1. A
2. C
3. B
4. B

ANSWER KEY (cont.)

Week 22 (cont.)

Day 4
1. C
2. B
3. D
4. D
5. A

Day 5
Responses will vary.

Week 23

Day 1
1. B
2. B
3. D
4. C

Day 2
1. B
2. D
3. B
4. C

Day 3
1. B
2. B
3. D
4. C

Day 4
1. C
2. A
3. C
4. A
5. D

Day 5
Responses will vary.

Week 24

Day 1
1. B
2. C
3. C
4. B

Day 2
1. D
2. B
3. C
4. B

Day 3
1. C
2. C
3. C
4. D

Day 4
1. D
2. B
3. B
4. C
5. C

Day 5
Responses will vary.

Week 25

Day 1
1. B
2. D
3. C
4. C

Day 2
1. A
2. C
3. D
4. C

Day 3
1. A
2. A
3. A
4. C

Day 4
1. D
2. C
3. D
4. C
5. D

Day 5
Responses will vary.

Week 26

Day 1
1. A
2. C
3. D
4. C

Day 2
1. C
2. A
3. B
4. D

Day 3
1. B
2. C
3. C
4. A

Day 4
1. C
2. C
3. A
4. A
5. B

Day 5
Responses will vary.

Week 27

Day 1
1. C
2. A
3. B
4. D

Day 2
1. B
2. A
3. D
4. B

Day 3
1. B
2. B
3. C
4. A

ANSWER KEY *(cont.)*

Week 27 *(cont.)*

Day 4
1. B
2. D
3. A
4. C
5. C

Day 5
Responses will vary.

Week 28

Day 1
1. A
2. C
3. C
4. D

Day 2
1. B
2. B
3. A
4. B

Day 3
1. D
2. C
3. B
4. A

Day 4
1. C
2. D
3. C
4. B
5. C

Day 5
Responses will vary.

Week 29

Day 1
1. D
2. C
3. D
4. D

Day 2
1. B
2. B
3. B
4. A

Day 3
1. A
2. B
3. C
4. D

Day 4
1. B
2. C
3. D
4. C
5. B

Day 5
Responses will vary.

Week 30

Day 1
1. B
2. D
3. C
4. A

Day 2
1. C
2. A
3. B
4. A

Day 3
1. D
2. C
3. B
4. A

Day 4
1. B
2. A
3. A
4. C
5. C

Day 5
Responses will vary.

Week 31

Day 1
1. B
2. B
3. C
4. D

Day 2
1. B
2. B
3. D
4. C

Day 3
1. D
2. C
3. C
4. D

Day 4
1. C
2. B
3. C
4. A
5. B

Day 5
Responses will vary.

Week 32

Day 1
1. C
2. B
3. D
4. B

Day 2
1. A
2. A
3. D
4. D

Day 3
1. C
2. B
3. C
4. C

ANSWER KEY *(cont.)*

Week 32 *(cont.)*

Day 4
1. A
2. C
3. B
4. C
5. A

Day 5
Responses will vary.

Week 33

Day 1
1. B
2. A
3. B
4. B

Day 2
1. C
2. C
3. C
4. D

Day 3
1. B
2. C
3. B
4. C

Day 4
1. C
2. B
3. B
4. C
5. B

Day 5
Responses will vary.

Week 34

Day 1
1. C
2. D
3. A
4. A

Day 2
1. B
2. C
3. A
4. C

Day 3
1. D
2. B
3. C
4. C

Day 4
1. C
2. D
3. B
4. B
5. D

Day 5
Responses will vary.

Week 35

Day 1
1. B
2. B
3. C
4. A

Day 2
1. B
2. A
3. A
4. D

Day 3
1. A
2. D
3. A
4. C

Day 4
1. B
2. A
3. A
4. C
5. D

Day 5
Responses will vary.

Week 36

Day 1
1. C
2. A
3. B
4. C

Day 2
1. C
2. C
3. B
4. C

Day 3
1. D
2. B
3. B
4. B

Day 4
1. A
2. C
3. B
4. D
5. B

Day 5
Responses will vary.

REFERENCES CITED

Marzano, Robert. 2010. When Practice Makes Perfect…Sense. *Educational Leadership* 68 (3): 81–83.

National Reading Panel. 2000. Report of the National Reading Panel. *Teaching Children to Read: An Evidence-Based Assessment of the Scientific Research Literature on Reading and its Implication for Reading Instruction* (NIH Publication No. 00-4769). Washington, DC: U.S. Government Printing Office.

Rasinski, Timothy V. 2003. *The Fluent Reader: Oral Reading Strategies for Building Word Recognition, Fluency, and Comprehension.* New York: Scholastic.

———. 2006. Fluency: An Oft-Neglected Goal of the Reading Program. In *Understanding and Implementing Reading First Initiatives*, ed. C. Cummins, 60–71. Newark, DE: International Reading Association.

Wolf, Maryanne. 2005. *What is Fluency? Fluency Development: As the Bird Learns to Fly.* Scholastic professional paper. New York: ReadAbout. http://teacher.scholastic.com /products/fluencyformula/pdfs/What_is_Fluency.pdf (accessed June 8, 2007).

DIGITAL RESOURCES

Accessing the Digital Resources

The digital resources can be downloaded by following these steps:

1. Go to **www.tcmpub.com/digital**

2. Sign in or create an account.

3. Click **Redeem Content** and enter the ISBN number, located on page 2 and the back cover, into the appropriate field on the website.

   ISBN:
   9781425809232

4. Respond to the prompts using the book to view your account and available digital content.

5. Choose the digital resources you would like to download. You can download all the files at once, or you can download a specific group of files.

Please note: Some files provided for download have large file sizes. Download times for these larger files will vary based on your download speed.

CONTENTS OF THE DIGITAL RESOURCES

Teacher Resources

- Assessing Fluency
- Writing Rubric
- Practice Page Item Analysis Chart
- Student Item Analysis Chart

Student Resources

- Practice Pages

NOTES